Tales from a
Prairie Journal

Rita Jerram

Stairwell Books and Fighting Cock Press

Published by Stairwell Books and Fighting Cock Press

Stairwell Books
161 Lowther Street
York, YO31 7LZ

and

Fighting Cock Press
45 Middlethorpe Drive
York, YO24 1NA

Original Fighting Cock logo by Stanley Chapman

Tales from a Prairie Journal©2015 Rita Jerram, Stairwell Books and
Fighting Cock Press

ISBN: 978-1-939269-26-3

Printed and bound in the UK by Russell Press
Second Printing by Imprint Digital
Edited by Pauline Kirk
Cover photograph: Trevor Reeves
Cover art: Alan Gillott

In 1884 my grandmother left her rural Derbyshire village at the age of eighteen, to travel to Canada to join her fiancé.

She kept journals for most of her life, graphically describing the many hardships and heartbreak she experienced, but also portraying the deep love she came to have for her adopted country. I have tried to depict some of these experiences by imagining myself walking in her footsteps, and taking a degree of artistic liberty in the process.

Rita Jerram

Table of Contents

Waiting for William

With a hiss of steam and a screech of released breaks the 'Pacific Queen' pulled away. Freshly watered and fuelled, she continued her journey across the prairies and over the Rocky Mountains to her final destination of Vancouver.

I was left alone, a solitary figure on the deserted wooden platform, tin trunk and wicker basket at my feet. As the train sped out of sight I lifted my hand to wave farewell, and remained so until it had become just a distant rumble, and no longer visible. Already I mourned its friendly warmth, the constant buzz of conversation, and the aroma and shared intimacy of my fellow passengers. I missed the security of the carriage which had sheltered me for the last five days, and most of all the thrill of travelling the Canadian Pacific Railroad.

The train had taken me across magnificent country, spanning rivers and deep canyons, cutting its passage through dense towering forests, and then crossing the seemingly endless prairies, dwarfed by their size and splendour. It had stopped at isolated halts to take on fuel and water, allowing weary passengers the chance to stretch their legs, and buy food from the railroad cook, who would set up his mobile wood stove at the side of the track. But I was now at my journey's end, and as the train shuddered to a stop the guard yelled out: "Blue River Halt, anyone for Blue River." This was my destination, the end of weeks of travel, and I felt suddenly afraid, and for the first time doubted my judgement in embarking on this pursuit.

It took only a matter of minutes to determine that there was no one to meet me. Blue River Halt consisted of the small wooden platform that I was standing on, a rusting water tank, a towering heap of logs, and a dusty wooden bench. A crumbling sign stated the population to be twenty-nine living souls, but someone had painted a line through the nine and replaced it with a five. Looking around this desolate spot I was vastly relieved to know that somewhere out there I would find at least twenty-five other living souls.

I sat on the bench and gazed out across the prairie – it was empty, no sign of any habitation, no sight of man or beast, just an endless stretch of land as far as my eyes could see. The midday sun shimmered and blurred the horizon. It looked beautiful, but also threatening, and very lonely.

I had never been so alone before; the utter silence was almost deafening. I wanted to shout and scream to fill the empty void of

1

isolation that surrounded me. The rail track, glinting in the sun, seemed to mock with its promise in either direction. I turned and scanned the landscape once again, searching for any sign of change, still hopeful that he would come.

I'd telegraphed him from Montreal, telling of my arrival in Canada, and giving the date and expected time that I would reach Blue River. As I sat waiting my mind drifted to home – I imagined my mother and sisters busy with their household chores, my father and brothers working the land; I wondered if the dogs still howled at the door, looking for my return. I had gone against my parents' wishes in following my fiancé to Canada, and I had left without their blessing. This saddened me, but had not swayed my determination to leave.

It had been three long years since William had emigrated – the younger son of a tenant farmer, he had been hungry for his own land. The great open spaces of the colony had tempted him away, promising to send for me when he was established. My patience had worn thin, and being young, headstrong, and very much in love, I had decided to make my own way to join him. But now with each passing moment the chill of doubt came over me, suspicion of his fidelity, and fears that his love had not remained true. It was difficult to recollect his face, and it had been so long that I too had some misgivings. My impulsive journey now seemed a terrible mistake.

I must have dozed awhile, a sudden coolness waking me. The sun had clouded over, and a breeze was beginning to waft across the open prairie. It was already late afternoon – I realised I had been waiting now for over four hours, and still no sign of him coming.

I was feeling anger against his neglect, and also apprehensive of nightfall. It seemed as if I was the only living person left in this great expansive land, and I felt defenceless and abandoned in such a solitary place. From the safety of the train I had seen packs of fearless wolves outrunning us on the tracks, and I'd heard tales of grizzly bears and wild coyotes who attacked lone travellers. I was afraid, and started to weep, and also prayed a little to gain some courage – *Why doesn't he come?*

Suddenly, through my tears, I saw a distant cloud of dust. I thought it at first a mirage, or perhaps a miracle in answer to my prayer. For another hour I watched the dust cloud approach, screwing up my eyes to form its shape, and at last I made out the outline of horses and wagon travelling at breakneck speed. I no longer cared if it was He, I just needed to see another human face, hear a voice, be it rapist or murderer. But I smoothed my skirt, rubbed the dust from my boots, and spat on a handkerchief to wipe the tears and smuts off my face, just in case it was him.

As the sweating horses neared, the wagon driver stood up on his seat, one hand on the reins, the other waving his hat in the air. I heard my name called, and despite the darkening sky and the veil of dust about him I could see it was my William, taller and broader than I remembered, but the same twinkling green eyes and mischievous smile.

He pulled to a halt, leapt from the wagon and gathered me tightly in his arms, kissing my trembling mouth until I was breathless. All the anger and fear of my long wait dissolved, I was so happy and relieved to see him.

He lifted me and my baggage onto the wagon, tenderly wrapping a blanket around my legs for protection from the cold prairie night, and then holding me close he turned the horses, and in a more sedate trot we set off, heading into the setting sun for my new home in the wilderness.

Blue River. 1st of May 1884.

The Homestead

The journey from Blue River Halt back to William's place seemed to take forever. A bright moon illuminated the mile after mile of grassy track as we drove across the prairie, open land that seemingly stretched to touch the starlit sky. I felt overwhelmed by the silent splendour of it all, and snuggled closer to William, pulling the rug tighter as the cold air made me shiver – or maybe it was the feelings of trepidation that were growing inside me as we sped nearer to our destination. The enormity of my escapade was slowly dawning on me: headstrong and always wilful, I'd given no heed to my parent's disquiet when I announced my plans to join William in Canada – and no thought at all to the possibility that he might not be overjoyed by my arrival.

I had talked incessantly for the first hour of our journey, telling him all the news of home and any local gossip that I thought would interest him. But then an uneasy silence fell between us – he was quieter than I remembered, as if the vastness of his surroundings had overpowered his previous liveliness. I could sense that he had changed. He seemed older, more serious, a grown man rather than the boy that had courted me back home. Despite this change in him I liked the feel of his strong arm around my shoulders, and the warmth of his muscular thigh next to mine.

I must have dozed and missed the boundary posts that were the start of William's land, because he was gently rousing me to point out the outline of his homestead, still some distance away but clearly visible in the early dawn light. The horses, sensing food, increased their pace – I sat up straighter, eager to glimpse my new home, and very conscious of William's pride in his property, and the huge achievements he had made since coming to this wild empty land.

As we grew closer I could make out a single storey log cabin and alongside it the shell of a half-built barn, which in the gathering light looked menacing as it towered over the yard. William halted the wagon in front of the cabin, tied the horses to the porch, and lifted me to the ground, tightening his hold as I stumbled, my limbs being weak and stiff from the long journey.

He helped me up the three steps that led on to the wooden porch, which ran the length of the cabin. "Welcome home," he said, and rather sheepishly begged me not to expect too much. Full of apology he told me it was not really suitable for female company, too small and not yet finished, but he gave his assurances that he would soon enlarge and improve it now that I had arrived. Taking hold of his hand I smiled at him and pushed open the unlocked door. The interior was poorly lit by one small window, and as my eyes became used to the dimness I could see all that my new home had to offer. Shabby, William had called it; at first glance I thought primitive a better choice of word. The walls were the inner side of the rough-hewn timber that made up the outer shell, and the pungent smell of the unseasoned wood pervaded the whole room. A rusting range stood against one wall, its tall chimney pipe thrusting its way through the tin roof. A sturdy, crafted table and two stools were set alongside a trestle bench, which held some scant utensils and a chipped wash bowl. Close by the stove was a crude pallet bed piled high with rugs and furs.

I was horrified that this was to be my home, and I was just about to turn to William and express my dismay, when I suddenly caught a glimpse of the wild flowers that were arranged in an old jar and placed in the centre of the table. They had so obviously been put there for my benefit that I held back my scathing words, and turned to him, giving a hug and kiss and praising his thoughtful gesture.

The horses needed to be fed and watered, and he had other chores to do, so I said I was well able to explore and familiarise myself with the cabin without his help. Once I had heard his footsteps leave the porch I sank down on the pallet bed in total despair. I wept bitter tears as I looked around me – there was little enough to see. I had not expected such hardship; the limitations of both the sea voyage and the train now seemed like utter luxury. My heart sank as the truth became obvious. William had not been ready to have me come, he'd been too busy working his land to think of preparing for a bride, and I had selfishly disregarded this, only thinking of my own needs.

Wiping away my tears, I felt anger against myself for being so arrogant, and for my pathetic show of weakness. I was here now, and there was no going back. I loved William, and would work alongside him to make a home to be proud of, and with a new determination I rose to my feet, rolled up my sleeves, raked the fire in the range and set the kettle to boil.

I could see that a visit to the trading post would be high on my list of jobs, with an urgent need for more crockery and household goods if I was to cook and clean. I noticed that William's clothes were hanging from a nail on the door; mine would have to stay in the trunk a while longer.

My wicker basket contained a few mementos I'd brought from home, so I took out a picture of my family and placed it on the floor next to the bed. I would ask William to fashion me a shelf to keep it on. The family group looked solemn, and seemed out of place here in a log cabin in the wilds of Canada – I wondered if I would ever see any of them again.

As night fell we sat at the table sharing a meal made from the meagre supplies I had found in the food safe. Earlier William had shown me the well that he'd recently dug at the back of the cabin, proud that we had a plentiful supply of good clean water. We were both tired, and sat quietly after our supper was finished, feigning a casual attitude, but very conscious of each other's presence. The solitary candle and the glow of burning wood in the range were casting shadows around the room, which in my tired and fanciful state made it look frightening. It was an awkward silence that neither knew how to break. At last William stood up, cleared his throat and said he would go outside and sleep in the wagon. Taking his rifle and a rug he bid me a shy goodnight and left the cabin.

I quickly undressed, blew out the candle and climbed into the pallet bed, pulling a rug and the furs over me, reminding myself that in the morning I must add sheets to my urgent shopping list. Weary as I was, sleep evaded me, and I lay in the darkness listening to the strange sounds of the night: the crackling of the logs in the range, and the sound that the wind made as it whistled down the chimney pipe. I was almost asleep when the blood-curdling sound of wolves howling brought me to my senses; racing to the door I screamed for William to come back inside. I took his hand and led him to the bed, and as we lay in each other's arms I knew he was glad that I had come.

He told me months later that the pack of wolves I'd heard would have been many miles away, sound carrying far in the prairie night.

The Homestead. 2nd of May 1884.

Settling In

My life I think has changed for ever. I dearly love my William and have no regrets at coming here to be with him, but I'm finding everything very different to what I had imagined life in Canada to be like. Back in England the newspapers carried glowing testimonies as to what wonderful opportunities the colony offered, and recommended young couples to leave the old country behind and emigrate to the land of plenty.

It is certainly a most beautiful, diverse land, and you couldn't fail to be impressed by its spectacular scenery and wonderful natural terrain. But in reality there is also much on the prairies to try your endurance to its limit. The newspapers had made no mention of the horse flies and mosquitoes, both of whom seem to make me their prime target, and who take delight in swarming around anything left unattended. Such is their ferocity I have spent the whole of my first month covered in bites, causing my legs and face to swell alarmingly.

I had expected some hardships, but had been totally unprepared for the adjustments I am having to make. My family home back in Derbyshire is a large, comfortable farmhouse that has been in our ownership for three generations. We lived a simple rural life, but luxurious compared to the very basic, almost primitive circumstances that I now find myself in. I keep my discontent a secret from William, knowing that he had been concerned before my arrival that it was not the sort of home I was used to. He's working hard to build a scullery at the rear of the cabin, and took me to the trading store within days of my coming to purchase the things I had thought necessary for our comfort.

Farming on the prairies is unlike anything I have known before. It's a backbreaking job just to prepare the land for cultivation. Blue River's soil is sandy, and without regular watering is not productive. A farmer can work hard tilling his land, and sowing seed, only to have a drought during the summer which can cause the crops to miserably fail. Like all the other farming folk, William owes money to the seed merchants, and prays nightly for summer rain to fall, to save the crops and enable us to clear our debts after the harvest is safely in.

As we drove along the prairie tracks to the trading post I'd noticed derelict cabins and overgrown land, and William explained that many emigrants had been beaten by failed crops and had deserted their homesteads, to either return home or to look for work in the townships, although I had been told, when talking to other rail passengers on my journey here, that unemployment was high in the towns and cities. I had myself noticed men trying to leap on to the trains as they had slowed down when passing through remote stations, and was told that they were hobos, hitching rides across the country in search of work.

Back in England I had heard of groups of Canadian emigration agents, who toured the country urging people to emigrate to Canada, and extolling its benefits. They had made particular entreaties to the farming communities, offering plentiful land, and easily obtainable loans to buy it with. This was tempting to men scratching a living on rented farms, and to labourers who had no hope of bettering themselves in the Old Country. But, from what I have heard and seen with my own eyes since coming here has made me realise that they had not been entirely truthful.

I'm desperately missing everyone at home, having always been very close to my mother and sisters. It is only now that I am here that I fully realise the vast distance that parts us, and I fret that I will never see any of them again. But, despite these sad thoughts, and the unexpected hardships, I am glad that I'm here with William, and I am sure that by working hard we will make a success of both the farm, and our partnership.

The distance parting me from my family is in the present circumstances most fortunate, as both of my parents would be dismayed to know of my sleeping arrangements, having no perception of life on the prairies, and not realising that finding a cleric to perform a marriage service is not easy, and could involve a long wait for one to appear. I know my mother would be profoundly shocked, but I don't intend her to find out, that both William and I consider ourselves by prairie law to be already married.

Offsetting the many drawbacks of prairie life is the wonderful air, so clean and fresh that your lungs inhale as if they are breathing for the first time. And the feeling of freedom that the wide open space gives you is very liberating, and I never tired of the magnificent sunsets that are preceded by the most amazing cloud formations. William laughs at me when I stand on the veranda for hours simply gazing at the sky. He said I will grow used to them, but such is their beauty I don't think that possible.

In the short time I've been here we have been visited by most of our closest neighbours, all making excuses for their calls, either a loan of one of William's tools or to bring him a piece of bacon after a hog killing, but, mainly I think to take a look at me. They were all very civil, the womenfolk accepting coffee and oatcakes whilst the men stand out in the yard talking of farming matters. One lady I particularly liked, by the name of Mary McDonald, she was very kind, and understanding of my homesickness, and the bewilderment of my new life. She and James, her husband, have been out here for eight years, having emigrated from the Scottish Highlands when first married. They have a mischievous little boy and another baby on the way, plus two older lads who were from Mary's previous marriage, she having met James after she was widowed young. It did me a power of good to have a woman to talk with, and I feel sure we will be good friends.

From our conversation I learnt that there is a very active social life on the prairies despite the long distances between homesteads. She said that the prairie farmers hold regular barn dances to which everyone goes, and invited us to attend the next one that was to be held in their barn. I was comforted by her chatter, and the knowledge that I would be able to have some female companionship, having thought myself completely isolated from any feminine association. I'm slowly adjusting to being a prairie farmer's wife, which is what I am, in spite of the lack of clergymen.

William was overjoyed when I made some butter, the first he'd tasted for a long time. For the past week I'd been saving the cream that was skimmed off our milking cows' daily yield, it was stored in the ice box which was kept under the cabin, reached by a trapdoor let into the earthen floor. An ingenuous contraption that is invaluable in the early summer months, it is filled with the solid blocks of ice that were rescued before the winter thaw, and then packed in straw and placed into the foundations which are the coolest part of the cabin.

The problem with my making butter was in not having a churn to turn it in. But William, ever resourceful, fashioned me a wooden tub and fixed some beating paddles inside, and within the hour my butter was turning. And that night for supper we enjoyed warm bread straight from the stove, lavishly plastered with our own butter. I also attempted cream cheese which I had watched my mother make many times, squeezing the water from the curds, and hanging it over a bowl pressed tight in one of my cotton stockings to await its souring. I have pickled large cucumbers which are plentiful and cheap to buy, and using my mother's recipes have made wild cherry jam, apple preserve and green tomato chutney. I am well pleased with my efforts, and intend writing my mother of their success. William was well pleased with the improvement to his diet, and hugged me, saying how glad he was that I had come out to join him.

9

In fact I am feeling more content, and despite the heat of summer, and the wretched horse flies, I'm beginning to appreciate my life on the prairies.

The Homestead, Blue River. 4th of June 1884.

A Prairie Wedding

Yesterday was my wedding day. At long last, a travelling preacher had arrived in Blue River – six months we had waited for him to come. Since his arrival he'd been kept busy with many christenings, and the belated funeral service of a farmer who had been buried in the early fall.

I had been up at dawn, too excited to sleep. I'd boiled water on the range, determined to wash my hair, and to bathe all over on such a special day. I had carefully laid out the white muslin dress that I had brought with me from England, made especially for this day. It was creased from laying too long in my trunk, and I was upset to find mildew on the sleeves, but hoped my silk shawl would cover the damage. My hands had felt rough on the delicate material, the last few months of toiling on the land having coarsened them, so I worked some lard into my skin to soften it, and used the last of my precious rose water to smooth my face.

William had long been ready, looking smart in his new pants and a freshly laundered shirt. I'd kissed him, and remarked how handsome he looked before sending him out to harness the horses whilst I got dressed. Despite its creases my dress looked beautiful, and fortunately long enough to hide my shabby boots, my only ornament being a silver locket, given to me by my mother before I'd left home to come to Canada.

Thinking of my mother had brought a sudden rush of tears to my eyes, and with them the thoughts of how different my wedding day would have been back home. My sisters would have been bridesmaids, and my father would have proudly led me down the aisle of our village church. But here I would be marrying in front of strangers with no friends or kinsfolk by my side. I'd quickly put away these thoughts, and briskly wiped the tears from my face before going out into the yard in search of William.

He was waiting by the wagon, and the look in his eyes and his smile told me that he found my appearance to his liking. I was deeply touched to see that somehow he'd obtained a length of white ribbon which he had formed into a clumsy bow and tied to the back of the wagon. He'd also found time to pick a bunch of wild prairie flowers which he presented me with for my bridal bouquet. Helping me on to the wagon he gallantly kissed my hand, and said, "You look lovely Miss

11

Goodwin," and for the first time in months I felt well-groomed and desirable.

The Indian summer that we had been enjoying was almost at an end, but the sun shone as we followed the well-worn trail, and despite my earlier sadness I'd felt a sudden surge of happiness. My William's arm was around my waist, and as he urged the horses on heading for the McDonald's place I wouldn't have exchanged my seat next to him for anything.

We were the last to arrive, and the McDonald's yard was crowded with wagons. It looked as if the whole of Blue River's farming community had come to see us wed. The women, all dressed in their Sunday clothing were gossiping together in the shade, whilst their menfolk leant against the wagons talking of crops and comparing the quality of their horses, and everywhere there were hordes of swarming children, enjoying their freedom after lengthy journeys that had probably started before daylight.

There was a loud cheer as William and I turned into the yard. I'd felt flustered and overwhelmed by such a reception, being no longer used to large gatherings such as this. I'd blushed and waited for William to introduce me as I knew scant few of our guests. But I was made to feel welcome: the women surged forward to hug and kiss me, whilst the men shook William's hand and wished him well. My dress was much admired before Mary McDonald had taken my hand and led me into to their cabin to freshen up before the ceremony. She was a kindly woman who could see my embarrassment at so much attention, and was someone I already considered my friend. Being a few years older, and also our nearest neighbour, she had always kept a motherly eye on my welfare. It was she who had suggested we marry in her husband's recently finished barn.

The preacher was waiting for us in the coolness of the new building with his prayer book opened at the marriage service. Everyone crowded inside, the women and children sitting on hay bales, and the men standing at the back admiring the set of the solid pine beams of James McDonald's new barn. The sweet smell of the freshly cut timber had engulfed me as I entered on William's arm, and the dim interior with its high vaulted roof had given me the feeling of being in church, and I had no longer felt that anything was lacking on this my wedding day.

When we came out into the sunshine I was wearing the wide gold ring that William had surprisingly produced. I later found out that it had belonged to a neighbour's deceased mother-in-law, and he had exchanged it for one of our new calves. The wedding service had been brief, our vows quickly given; only I knew of the crossed fingers hidden under my silk shawl when I'd promised to obey, having always had a problem with that word.

Clean cloths were spread on to the grass and laid out with plentiful food. As prairie custom decreed, everyone had contributed to the wedding feast: we had cold wild turkey cooked in a seasoned gravy, home-cured baked ham, baskets of freshly picked sweet corn swimming in warm butter, and bread still hot from Mary's oven. After eating our fill the barn was cleared for dancing, an Irish neighbour took up his fiddle and soon our feet were tapping to his lively tunes. William and I led the dancing and soon everyone had joined in, young and old alike. It had felt strange when a young farm lad had asked William's permission to dance with his wife, and I sharply told him to ask me first, but I'd smiled at William when I said it.

Everyone was in good spirits. Prairie folk loved a good party and would travel miles for one, be it a wedding or funeral, or just an excuse to get together with their far-flung neighbours. It was always a welcome diversion from the loneliness of prairie life. Families bedded their children down in their wagons, and would talk or dance all night, often not heading back home until daybreak, reaching their homesteads in time for milking.

I was moved by their gestures of friendship, and grateful for the many simple wedding gifts that they had piled onto our wagon – jars of wild strawberry jam, various types of homemade chutney and even a full salted ham. Mary McDonald had given us a beautiful patchwork quilt that she had laboured on for many months. She promised to teach me the art of making one, a useful occupation she said, for the long winter months when housebound. This warmth and kindness from them all brought tears to my eyes, and made me feel that I was no longer a stranger in their midst.

At nightfall the men started to disappear behind the back of the barn, leaving the women and children to dance alone and we women guessed that the McDonald whisky still was hidden there, and as the drink flowed we could hear raised voices, with old grievances fuelled by the potent alcohol flared up – as they often did at prairie parties. Mary McDonald went to intervene, and within minutes the men had appeared back in the barn, somewhat sheepish and slightly unsteady on their feet, prepared once again to do their duty and dance with the ladies, and if occasionally two of them slipped away together for a secret tipple their wives discreetly failed to notice.

As the first sign of dawn came, people were still sat around telling jokes or sharing old stories, the children by now lay sleeping in the wagons or on the bales of straw in the barn, and the old people were nodding off where they sat. Only the young unattached men still strutted around the yard as they showed off to any eligible young ladies. Sadly there were always more men available on the prairie than women, and the young girls could afford to take their pick.

As the sky lightened we had said our goodbyes. William helped me on to the wagon as everyone came to wish us good fortune. I had smiled at his struggle to take the reins in his hands, as he'd also spent time behind the cabin and was not at his best, but I knew the horses would take us safely home. The trail, as they well knew, would take them back to their dinner trough.

Whilst leaning against my new husband, wrapped warmly under the shared blanket, I had suddenly felt our baby quicken – just as well, I thought, that the preacher had been.

Blue River. 5th of October 1884.

Cissie's Party

It was James McDonald who passed on the news of Cissie's birthday party. Invitations were usually delivered in this manner, the prairie grapevine being a very efficient way of conveying such information. He called whilst on his way to the trading post, and seemed eager for William to come over from the barn to hear the arrangements for himself. I was excited; this would be the first party that we would be attending as a married couple, and I had kept my wedding dress hanging on the door for just such an occasion.

Considering the vast distances between farms, I had been surprised to find such an active social scene. In our neighbourhood it seemed that any excuse was enough to throw a dance or a party. Winter's onset soon put a stop to prairie socialising, but on warm summer evenings there was much traffic on the grassy tracks between homesteads. It was a chance for the womenfolk to dress up a little, exchange gossip, and have some relief from the monotony of their daily lives, and for the men an opportunity to compare crop prices and the rigours of prairie farming. It was an open invitation to all – you were just expected to take a baked pie or two, and perhaps a keg of your home brew with you.

James McDonald had told us that Mr and Mrs Anderson were giving their only daughter, Cissie, a party that coming Saturday, to celebrate her eighteenth birthday. I had not yet met the Anderson family as they been unable to attend our wedding, and I said I was eager to meet Cissie as she was so near to my own age. I saw James Me Donald give William a sly look as I said it, but such was my excitement I thought little of it.

Come Saturday afternoon I'd washed and curled my hair, put my wedding dress and William's best over-shirt to air, and baked a tray of apple pies in readiness for the evening's entertainment. As the afternoon crept on there was no sign of William's return from the fields, and much to my annoyance the sky was darkening before I heard him in the yard. I rushed outside fully dressed in my finery to berate him for being so late. "I have a headache," he said, "maybe I'm sickening for something, and perhaps it would be wiser not to go to the Anderson place." I felt his brow, which was perfectly cool to my touch, and his eyes were clear. He looked the picture of good health. I burst into tears, which totally unmanned him, and I'm ashamed to say that I stamped my foot and called him some beastly names, the disappointment taking the guard off my tongue. He said he was sorry and promised he would quickly clean up, and despite the late hour we would go to the party.

He was unusually quiet as we covered the miles between our place and Windy Ridge, the Anderson's homestead, and I was a little concerned in case he really was unwell. I took his hand and squeezed it to let him know there was no ill feeling between us, and he slipped his arm around my waist in return. The horses seemed familiar with the trail and plunged forward with little guidance from their driver, the reins being slack in his hand as we kissed and cuddled. I asked him what sort of girl Cissie was. "Just ordinary," he replied. "But is she pretty?" I wanted to know. "Fair enough," he said, "but not as beautiful as you," and with that he silenced me with more kisses. Satisfied I leant against him as we headed up the Anderson track towards the distant lights of the homestead.

We were the last to arrive, and as William fastened up the horses alongside the other wagons we could hear the buzz of conversation and laughter coming from the lit barn where the party was being held. I might have been mistaken, but I felt a definite hush when we entered, and William put his arm protectively around my shoulders as we crossed the barn to greet the Anderson family.

Edward and Lillian Anderson pushed through the throng of silent neighbours to welcome us. "We had given you up for lost," Mr Anderson said, after heartily shaking William's hand and kissing me on the cheek. His wife swiftly averted her face as she acknowledged our greeting, "It's been a long time since we had the pleasure of your company at Windy Ridge, William, but you and your new wife are welcome." She smiled but her eyes were cold and belied her words. I felt her looking at the tightness of my dress and the faint swell of my stomach, and sensed her disapproval. I turned away and saw a girl of about my height and age coming towards us. She was slight of build, with delicate features, and wavy sandy-coloured hair, and the pale freckled skin that goes with it. She was smiling and gracious as she held out her hand to greet us. "Hello Cissie," William quietly said. She blushed from face to chest as fair people often do, and gave him a shy hug. He introduced us and I handed her the crocheted shawl I had made as a birthday gift. She thanked me and I impulsively pulled her to me and said I hoped we would be friends. She gave me a strange look, almost as if I was insulting her, and then turned away. The fiddler took up his bow and started to play a lively tune and William hastily took me in his arms before I could start to question her odd behaviour, and waltzed me around the barn floor, making me too breathless to speak.

16

I put my hurt feelings aside and enjoyed the pleasure of dancing with my husband. Others joined us and soon dust was swirling from the mud-packed floor. Later in the evening, when William had disappeared with the other men to sample the Anderson still, I stepped outside to get a welcome breath of air. It was a beautiful evening, the sky was full of sparkling stars and I thought it the prettiest sight I had ever seen. Two women whom I had never met before were sitting on hay bales, their heads together, quite unaware of my presence in the shadows, both scandal gossiping, as women do when thinking themselves alone. "I don't know how he dare show his face," one of them savagely said, "that poor girl is broken-hearted." "She's better off without him," the other one replied, "as good as jilted she was. Every Sunday, regular as clockwork, he turned up for his supper – she had every reason to think him serious." I stepped out of the darkness to go back into the barn. Both were startled to see me and looked at each other, aghast at being overheard.

When the men came back inside I idly wondered which one's ears had been burning during the conversation I'd overheard. But it was time to cut the birthday cake and William came to my side whilst Cissie blew out her candles and made her wish. I wondered what she was wishing for, perhaps a handsome husband like mine, and I lovingly stroked his arm, happy to be his wife and basking in his love.

The dancing resumed and the fiddler called for two circles to be made, the women in the inner one and the men in the outer. We circled the barn floor in silence and when the music started, danced with the partner opposite. I soon lost William as the circles moved on and ended up dancing with a tall, gangly Swede who spoke little English. I saw Cissie in my husband's arms, dreamily dancing, with such a look of bliss on her face that I had an immediate flash of enlightenment. I realised she was in love with him, and understood at once the furtive looks and the gossip I'd overheard. She had obviously thought him courting her, but then I had come along and her hopes were shattered. I felt pity as I watched her gazing up at him with unashamed adoration in her eyes. Then I felt anger, a raging anger that he had dared to bring me here without my knowing anything of this previous relationship, how people must be laughing at me. I flushed at the memory of asking her to be my friend. I also understood now William's reluctance to come, the sour look on Mrs Anderson's face and also the neighbours knowing looks. I felt so humiliated I could have killed him.

As soon as the dance had finished I abandoned my place in the circle and went across the floor to him; he could see by my flashing eyes and angry stance that trouble was brewing, and quickly led me to a quiet area at the back of the barn. I calmly said I was not feeling well and would like to go home – immediately! He hastily made our farewells and tried to take me by the hand, but I pushed him away, much to the amusement of the watching onlookers, and with my head held high, but also very close to tears, I marched out, leaving William to make his apologies.

Following close behind he made to lift me on to the wagon, but I angrily pulled away and despite my skirts clambered up by myself, my figure stiff and unforgiving as he climbed on to the seat next to me. He gathered the reins and let the horses have their head, as anxious as I to put a distance between us and Cissie's party.

As soon as we were on the trail and out of sight and earshot of the Anderson place I turned and slapped his face, and the horses all but bolted at the sudden sharp sound it made.

"How dare you take me to that girl's party," I yelled at him.

"But it was you who threw a tantrum to go," he replied.

"But I didn't know you had been courting her," I threw back at him, and raised my hand to strike again. He drew the horses to a halt and tried to take me in his arms but I resisted, and, screaming abuse at him, attempted to climb down from the wagon. Hanging on to my skirt he tried to calm me, explaining that it had all been a misunderstanding. "I was lonely," he said, "and they were a friendly family who welcomed me, it was good to sit round their table on a Sunday evening, having home-cooked food, it reminded me of home, and Cissie knew I was engaged, we were just good friends."

"Just good friends," I spat at him, "when it's plain to see the girl is besotted with you, and worst of all everybody knows it. They must think me a fool for being the only one not to know, and laughing at me for asking her to be my friend."

He took my hand and turned me towards him, holding my face close to his, and said, "I love you dearly you little shrew, and will never want another." Looking into his eyes I knew he was sincere and I softened a little towards him, but still held back, the evening's hurt feelings staying raw.

The horses were champing to go home and so we drove the rest of the way in silence, until within a few miles of our boundary I could stand his sadness no more, and I took his hand and held it against my face. Laying down the reins and leaving the horses to make their own way, he took me in his arms and held me as if he would never let me go again. Snuggled up next to him, and secure against his familiar body, I knew he had not let me down with Cissie, but part of me also knew that I'd come out to Canada just in time.

Blue River. 27th of October 1884.

A Prairie Wake

On one of our regular visits to the trading post to collect our mail and buy necessary provisions, we heard the sad news that old Joe Murphy had passed away. William was sorry, having known him well, and in fact, had lodged with him when first arriving in the Province, and had appreciated the old man's knowledge and help when taking up his own place. I had only met him once, but remembered him tirelessly playing the fiddle at our wedding a few weeks back.

We decided to carry on up the trail and attend his burial which was to be that very day on his homestead in Blue River Gap. In truth, I didn't really have any feelings about his demise, but was always eager for any change in the monotony of our daily lives. It would be an opportunity to meet up with the neighbourhood women – I longed to ask their advice about my swollen ankles, and the permanent backache that being with child had brought me.

As we neared the gap we met up with others, all heading for the Murphy place. The track was taking on a festive air with cheerful greetings exchanged between the wagons as each followed the well-worn trail, most folk in their working clothes as we were, all having left their farm chores to attend the burial.

Everyone knew that old Joe had no kin to mourn him, and many had travelled long distances to show him some respect and solidarity. Few of us had close family, all having left home and our roots in some other land to settle in this untamed country, but we all realised the importance of unity, and the need to create some sense of belonging in the small community that we shared, although I think some of the women, like I, would have come with an urgent need to see a friendly face, for which any excuse would have done.

No preacher was available, but the menfolk dug a grave, and old Joe was laid to rest in a hastily put together coffin, but with proper respect, and the Lord's Prayer reverently said over him. Afterwards the men went into the barn to share out old Joe's tools and livestock. It seemed mercenary, but such was the custom of the prairie.

Old Joe, so far as was known, had no wife or children to put a claim on his possessions – in fact very little was known of him at all, but then on the prairie great store was placed on a man's right to privacy, no questions were asked, your past was unimportant, and you were accepted for what you were. No one even knew old Joe's age, or where he'd come from, although when he was fuelled by alcohol, which it was claimed he often was, he would sing Irish ballads, his favourite ones being 'Danny Boy' and the 'The Irish Rover', so people felt safe in thinking him Irish despite his cultured English accent. There was talk of him having been an army man, and there had been something military in his bearing. His tongue was often loosened by drink, but he never divulged his past.

Over the years his farm had been neglected and had fallen into some disrepair, but it was good land, and would be quickly taken. He'd always had an Indian woman to cook and clean for him, and people whispered that she'd had other duties too. There had been no sign of her at the burial, and as old Joe's good horse had gone missing, it was assumed she'd gone back to her own people. Some of the men wanted to fetch the horse back, but were convinced by their womenfolk to let it go, no sense in stirring up trouble with the Indians – and anyway, we all thought she had most likely earned it.

This being my first prairie death I was somewhat embarrassed by the ritual of sharing out the deceased possessions. Whilst the men were bartering over a milking cow and her two calves, the women were in the cabin sharing out pots and pans, and dividing grubby linen into equal piles. I refused my share, and declined to pick out anything else from the few household articles that had not already been appropriated. But, as I turned to leave I saw an old tea caddy discarded by the scavengers, I presumed because of its poor condition. It was the faded picture on the lid that attracted my attention, a hand painted scene of an English country village that reminded me of home, and as no one else seemed interested in it I decided to take it as a memento of old Joe.

With everything arranged to everyone's satisfaction it was time to head for home, where stock would need feeding and watering, and countless other chores awaiting our return – life for the rest of us had to go on. The menfolk were very talkative and merry, having found old Joe's hidden still, and his stash of moonlight whiskey. They'd drank a toast to him, and then another, and if we women hadn't intervened they would have carried on until they'd drunk it dry. We sharply reminded them of their responsibilities and the sad occasion that we had come for. Shamefaced and none too steady on their feet, they reluctantly headed back to their wagons, goodbyes were said, and we all set off together down the trail, the wagons loaded with their spoils, and old Joe's livestock tethered behind them.

William was happy to have got a rifle, a beauty he said, that always fired straight and true, we also got a great big slobbering dog that nobody else would take, and which would have been left to roam wild or be killed by wolves.

Later that night I took out my tea caddy and admired its colours under the lamplight. I forced open its lid and tipped the contents out on to the table and found a faded picture of a beautiful women, inscribed 'to my darling Joseph,' another smaller half torn photograph was of a serious looking baby staring wide-eyed at the camera, its other side bearing the inscription 'Elizabeth aged six months,' and a blonde curl taped underneath. Some yellowing newspaper cuttings crumbled under my fingers, but enough remained to give the story of an army officer's court martial, and the verdict – guilty of killing his wife's lover. Another crumbled cutting had a picture of an upright man in uniform looking grim and sad, and despite its age it had a look of old Joe.

I gathered them up and put them in the stove, and watched the flames devour a life that had been discarded. The man was dead, he'd paid the price and now deserved his privacy. I filled the caddy with tea and placed it on my shelf.

Blue River. 3rd of November 1984.

Christmas on The Prairie

My spirits were low as the Christmas season approached. This would be my first away from home and family, and I was sorely distressed by their absence.

The festive season back home would be well under way by now. My mother would have had her mincemeat and puddings made by early October, and the Christmas cake baked, and drizzled with brandy before the month was out. My father would have had a pig killing, with its hams already curing in saltpetre on the cool stone slabs in the larder, and the two lean sides of bacon hanging from the smoke blackened kitchen beams.

A goose would be fattening in the yard, unaware that its end was due on Christmas Eve, when Mother would chase it around the yard with a chopper hidden in her apron pocket. She would wring its neck, chop off the head and sit out in the wash house to pluck it. We always laughed to see her sitting there in a white snowstorm of feathers.

My brothers would go into the woods in search of a tree that we all decorated on Christmas morning, and they would also drag back a great log to burn on the parlour fire. My sisters and I scoured the hedge-growth for red berried holly, and scanned the orchard trees for a spray of mistletoe. It was under the mistletoe that William first snatched a kiss, my sisters giggling at his boldness, but my father frowning at such brazen behaviour – despite our engagement having been celebrated two months past.

Come Christmas Eve the whole family, including domestic staff and the farm workers, would attend midnight service in the village church. Afterwards we would link arms and walk home down the frosty lane, the men carrying lanterns, and all of us singing carols. Back at the farm my father always invited the farm labourers into the kitchen for a glass of mulled wine, and one of my mother's mince pies. Afterwards each worker would be given a golden sovereign, a piece of ham, and some tobacco to take home. If they were married, my mother would hand them a Christmas pudding and a new shawl for their wives. The live-in staff had their sovereign too, and a length of cloth to make new Sunday clothing.

Christmas day we always had our meal at noon, and exchanged gifts as we sat around the big kitchen table. Later in the day, after afternoon milking was done, our close relatives would arrive and stay for supper. The older generation would sit in the parlour where Aunt Ellie would play the piano, but we younger ones would stay in the kitchen and tell jokes, and play charades. Later, William and I would sit on the fireside settle in the dimmest part of the room, and he would put his arm across my shoulder, and gently stroke my hair, and I, greatly daring, would put my hand upon his knee. His close presence would agitate me, and arouse feelings that made me blush. If mother or father came into the kitchen we would quickly move apart. After supper and prayers everyone would leave; we had early bedtimes on the farm, and Christmas day was no exception.

And now it was Christmas Eve here on the prairies, and I sat alone in front of the stove, weeping. As I sat, I think I really understood for the first time the enormity of my leaving home and kin to come out here to William. But I'd followed my heart, and here I was. I dried my tears and started to prepare supper, but with a heavy heart. We had planned to take up the kind invitation that the McDonald family had given us, and spend Christmas day at their place. But the weather had changed, and from an earlier slight flurry of snow we were now experiencing heavy falls, the track was hardly visible, and I knew William wouldn't risk the horses on such a journey.

He had gone out to the barn to milk the cow and feed the stock, he seemed to be overlong, and I was worried that he might have slipped in the icy yard. I was just putting on my shawl and lighting a lamp to go in search of him, when I heard his step on the porch. He pushed open the door and dragged in the largest spruce tree I'd ever seen, its top brushing against the cabin's roof. It was beautiful, with icicles hanging from its boughs like magical sparkling candles. I clapped my hands with excitement and ran to help William set it upright in the washtub. He hugged me and whispered 'Happy Christmas' as we stood back to admire it, and then to laugh, as the magical icicles rapidly melted with the heat of the stove. We spent the remainder of the evening making shapes from magazines to decorate its splendour, and later, when lying in each other's arms, smelling the pungent smell of pine, I knew I was happy to spend Christmas here in our little cabin with the man I loved.

Blue River. Christmas 1894.

Visitors

When I first saw the two riders heading down the track I thought they must be neighbours on their way to the trading post, and making a detour to see how I was. I quickly put fresh coffee on the stove, and exchanged my soiled apron for a clean one, then smoothing back my hair I sat on the porch eagerly awaiting their arrival. I was truly in need of company, William having been away these past two weeks working northwards with the rail gang. With a baby coming and seed to buy for next spring's planting, we needed the extra money he would earn.

I was often lonely, but never afraid of being left alone on the homestead. I loved the peace and tranquillity of my surroundings, revelling in the vast grandeur of its sweeping acres, but I also looked forward to the occasional visits from our neighbours. As the riders reached the gate I searched the horizon but could see no wagon following behind them, and was a little disappointed that no womenfolk were coming. I would have liked to have talked of my coming confinement, having a host of questions, and fears that only a woman could answer.

The two riders were almost in the paddock, and the dogs were fiercely barking. I stood up, shielding my eyes against the glare of the sun, but I had no recognition of either of them. One, tall and lean, with the look of a rogue about him, rode boldly right up to the porch steps, whilst the other who was squat and deathly pale had halted his horse some distance away, and as I stared, slumped forward across his mount as if in a faint. I felt apprehensive, but looked the tall one straight in the eye and asked him his business. He said they needed directions to Buffalo Gap, and the chance to water their horses. I told him I couldn't help with his request for direction, never having had the opportunity to visit there, and no certain knowledge of its route, but I would allow him to water his horses.

He asked if I was alone. I lied and said my husband was out in the fields and would soon be back for his dinner. He looked back at his companion who was still lying face down, and half slipping from his saddle. "He's pretty sick," he said. "I'd take it kindly, ma'am, if you'd let us rest awhile." Still dubious about them both, but also very conscious of upholding the unwritten rules of prairie hospitality, I invited them to sit on the porch. The tall man helped the sick one up the steps and sat him in my chair, where he fell backwards with his eyes closed. I told the tall one that I would get them some refreshments whilst he fed and watered the horses.

Coming out of the cabin with coffee, and some freshly baked corn bread, I was horrified to find the sick one lying on his back on the floor, with a trickle of blood seeping through his shirt front. My inclination was to run back inside and barricade the door, but at that moment the tall one came across the yard, and seeing my intention to flee, raced up the steps to stop me. I didn't take kindly to his restraint, but was persuaded to help him drag his wounded friend inside the cabin, and was dismayed by the slimy trail of blood that was left on my clean floor. By way of explanation the tall one said they had suffered a slight accident further up the trail when a gun had unfortunately backfired. I nodded acceptance of this unlikely tale, and continued to bathe the wound, which on close encounter seemed less serious than the loss of blood suggested. Despite my limited knowledge of shotgun injuries I could see that this one was a simple flesh wound. It looked as if a bullet had gouged the flesh and then sped on its way. I thought it best to stay silent and so kept my own counsel as I stemmed the flow of blood and tightly bound his chest with strips of linen reluctantly, I might add, torn from one of my trousseau sheets.

I had been long enough on the prairies to know better than to ask unnecessary questions. This vast province was still largely untamed and often lawless. I agreed to them staying a while, although I didn't feel I had much choice. Whilst they rested I prepared a parcel of food to give them when they left. As darkness fell they saddled the horses and prepared to leave, the squat one now having more colour in his face and seeming steadier on his feet. The tall one turned his horse at the gate and came back to press something into my hand, "For the little one, Ma'am," he said, before touching his hat and riding off into the night. Going back into the cabin I looked at what he'd given me and was shocked to see a small gold nugget lying in my outstretched palm.

I set to work to erase all evidence of their visit, scrubbing the porch and cabin floor until every trace of blood had gone, and then, feeling a sudden weakness that threatened to take my legs from under me, I sat down to rest and regain my composure. I must have nodded off because the barking of the dogs and a sudden banging at the door startled me. I was shocked to see a uniformed man standing on the porch, a revolver in his hand, and three more armed and mounted were in the yard. They asked if I'd seen two men that day, desperate men, who were wanted for a murder up north in Yellow Creek, where they had robbed and killed a prospector for his gold. He said they had been on their trail for over a week, almost catching the pair further up the track, and wounding one of them as they fled.

Fingering the gold nugget in my pocket I shook my head and said no one had been near the homestead that day, grateful as I lied for the darkness that hid my blushes, and the visitors' tracks. Another prairie rule I'd quickly learnt was to always keep silent when the Mounties call. We were a small community in Blue River and protected our own. I felt sorry for the murdered prospector and would remember him in my prayers, but I reasoned that the gold nugget was better in my pocket than in theirs.

They told me to bolt my door and open it to no one that night, and then they turned their horses and sped away – in entirely the wrong direction, as I noted from the cabin window.

When William returned home a few days later I said nothing of my visitors, or of the gold nugget which I'd hidden away, and was keeping for a rainy day.

Blue River. 20th of January 1885.

A Prairie Winter

My first winter on the prairie was far worse than I could have ever imagined. Eighteen years of England's changing seasons had done little to prepare me for the ferocity of a Canadian winter.

When first arriving at the homestead I'd been amazed at the sheer size of the timber stack which adjoined the cabin. It towered to the height of the roof and spread the breadth of its back, and despite the impressive amount of logs already stacked inside it, William had spent most of the fall sawing more. I innocently, and with some amusement, asked him if he was chopping enough to last our lifetime. He smiled and said his biggest fear was of not having enough when winter came.

We were also making weekly trips to the trading post, each visit seeing us laden down with what I thought of as excessive supplies of provisions, the wagon groaning under the weight of such extravagance. I teased William, and asked if he was expecting a siege. He just smiled again and told me to wait and see.

At this time the weather was still mild, and the gentle breezes that blew across the open land were pleasant after the summer heat. I was by now growing big with child, feeling lethargic and slow in movement, content to sit on the porch sewing for my coming baby, allowing William to make whatever winter precautions he felt needful.

When winter came it was sudden, with an icy blast that almost took my breath, the balmy days whipped away with a relentless, penetrating chill that seemed to freeze flesh to bone. Overnight the green expanse of land was dressed by a glistening frost, totally unlike the frost back home: this was a searing coldness that froze your hand to the door, bringing tears to your eyes that formed miniature icicles as they trickled down your cheek.

The range roared furiously, burning logs night and day. William pushed our bed pallet nearer to its warmth, and at nightfall fastened a wooden shutter over the window, but still we were cold. We piled clothes on to clothes, forgot about personal cleanliness as our water was too precious to waste, every drop laboriously melted from the ice, our well having long since frozen over. With the first onset of winter William had moved the livestock into the barn, and struggled twice a day, slipping and sliding across the yard to attend to their needs, coming back frozen to the marrow, his gloved hands frosted to the milk churn, and his face taut from the icy coldness that threatened to invade the cabin each time he opened the door.

The days were short, with an early darkness that seemed to invade my spirit, leaving me gloomy and depressed, and I worried that the baby would be affected by the blackness of my mood. As the winter took its hold we both became subdued, communicated less, and lost the easy relationship we had previously known.

Time seemed to have stood still. Our sole priority was to keep the range fed with logs, which it devoured with a frightening ferocity – I felt ashamed of my previous mockery of William, realising now the need behind his compulsive sawing and chopping. In a winter such as this, our very lives were dependent on the preparations he had made.

It had snowed heavily since Christmas, and the frequent snowstorms made it impossible for us to leave the farm, or for anyone to visit us. The track was no longer visible, lost beneath a flawless carpet of snow that stretched as far as the eye could see, the dazzling whiteness blinding and distorting your conception of the land's utter remoteness.

During one such snowstorm we were roused from our bed by the dogs fiercely barking. William took up his rifle and forced open the door, battling the drifting snow that had piled high on the porch, where it had reached the window, blocking out the light, and confusing our already muddled perception of night and day. A sorry figure fell onto the steps, snow-covered from head to toe, his bushy eyebrows and beard glistening with ice. He was in no condition to be a threat, so William laid down his rifle and helped him inside.

He lay on the floor in front of the range, unable to speak or even move his frozen limbs, and whilst William braved the snow drifts to take the stranger's horse to the barn, I cut away his frosted outer clothing, rubbed his chilled body with spirit, and piled covers over him to still his shaking limbs. After a bowl of hot broth, and time spent in front of the range, he felt able to introduce himself; he was a French-Canadian from Quebec by the name of Jacque de Villier. He had been making his way across country to Buffalo Creek and had hoped to ride out the blizzard, but as it became more fierce he had lost the trail and had been wandering aimlessly for many hours. If our chimney smoke had not caught his eye, he would have surely died.

Jacque stayed with us for nearly three weeks, the snowy weather never abating in that time. He was a pleasant fellow, but I found his constant presence difficult, and often felt uncomfortable with the situation. Our cabin was small, the one room our only habituation, the small scullery which had been hastily added after my arrival was not suitable as living space. I suffered deep embarrassment with our sleeping arrangements, and the meagre sanitary facilities that we shared. Without seeming petty, I also begrudged the decline in our rations; as winter stretched on endlessly the abundant provisions that William had been far-sighted enough to buy were, with an extra mouth to feed, lessening by the day.

He was friendly and entertaining, used to living rough, and not put out at all by seeing me in my nightwear. I think William really appreciated his company, having missed male conversation as much as I was missing a woman's. They shared a drink, and played endless games of poker well into the night, with me burrowing under the covers to shut out the sound of their raised voices as they joked and drank the hours away. He helped William shovel the snow each day to clear a path to the barn and wood pile, and in a brief respite they braved the cold and butchered one of our young steers, skinning it and hoisting the carcase high on to the cabin roof to protect it from hungry wolves. The freezing winds would keep it fresh for use till spring.

William had for many months been fashioning a crib for our coming baby, but I think it was a little beyond his carpentry skills, and he happily allowed Jacque the finishing touches. He was a true craftsman and made a crib fit for royalty. And as a gift for me, he made a sturdy nursing chair, polishing the wood to such a gloss that I could see my reflection on its seat.

My only real grievance was his swearing. His English, whilst not good, was fluent when using bad language, and I made my objections clear, as William well knew I would not sanction swearing in my house. Jacque, rogue that he was, started to swear in French, teaching William the basic necessary words. I must admit they sounded more poetical, and had a certain ring when used in anger.

The weather cleared quite suddenly one morning, still freezing cold, but with a clear blue sky that lifted my spirits, and took me out on to the porch for the first time in weeks. Jacque decided it was time for him to leave. He saddled his horse, clutched William to him in a manly hug, and then made me blush by lifting me off my feet, and kissing me on both cheeks. Taking the pack of food I'd prepared, he mounted his horse and rode off across the snow, heading in the direction that William had pointed out. I wished him well, but was relieved to see him go and to have the cabin to ourselves again. It seemed strangely quiet without him, and I felt shy around William for a while, but we were back to our usual compatibility by nightfall.

As the snows started to thaw, and green tufts of grass began to show, I felt more at ease with myself. I was nearing my time and William had fetched Mary McDonald to be at the birthing. I was happy to have her come; she reassured me as my own mother would have done. My sweet little girl was born two days later after a long hard labour. Between my pains I could hear William chopping wood in the yard, and I smiled at his choice of activity so early in the spring.

Mary McDonald praised me for my courage in the difficult birth, but professed her puzzlement at some of the words I'd used whilst enduring the more intense pain. "I was talking French," I said, and then closed my eyes and slept.

Blue River. 18th of March 1895.

Lizzie's Christening

By the time the travelling preacher arrived back in Blue River, Lizzie had already celebrated her second birthday, and I was nearing my time with a second child. I had hoped his visit would be delayed a while – it would be more timely to have both children christened together, as it could be another two years before he reached these parts again.

With Blue River rapidly increasing its population, he was going to have a busy time of it this visit. I knew of two couples who were waiting to wed, and there were any amount of graves to be blessed, plus at least a dozen children to christen, my Lizzie being one of them. William had left word for him at the trading post on our last trip there.

A few days later Eddie Wilk's errand boy came out to the homestead bearing a message from the preacher. He was running short of time it seemed, and suggested that he would find it most helpful if our little community would allow him to christen all the Blue River children together in one place, rather than have him travel from farm to farm. Taking in account my delicate condition, he was suggesting that our place be used as an appropriate venue.

I was very happy with this idea. William was worried that with my time so near it would be too tiring for me, but I assured him I could cope and would in fact enjoy it. He bid the boy to inform the preacher, and to ask Eddie Wilks to let everyone involved know that our barn would be cleared and ready for the following Sunday. But he warned that if a party was wanted they would have to organise it amongst themselves, his wife being indisposed.

I felt embarrassed at his remarks, and ashamed that people might be offended at our lack of hospitality, but William assured me that the neighbours would understand, all being well aware of my condition; he was adamant that I must rest and not agitate myself about the affair.

Come Sunday the sun was shining, and we looked set to have a good day. The barn was swept and ready, and I'd spread a white embroidered cloth across a bale of hay to serve as an altar table, and Lizzie and I had picked flowers to decorate the doorway. William had contributed some homemade beer, and opened up the whisky still that was usually hidden behind the wood store.

Much to his annoyance I'd been on my feet since early morning, baking bread, and making griddle scones, and now I was burdened with a nagging painful back ache, although I was not going to admit this to him. I sat out on the porch with Lizzie on my knee, and dressed her in a pretty crocheted smock that I had saved for this day. Just as well I thought, that the preacher had come: she was growing so fast it scarcely met across her back. As I tried to coax some curls into her unruly hair I saw the first of the wagons coming down the track, and prayed the back ache would soon go, as I wanted to enjoy my daughter's special day.

Soon the yard was full of wagons, and whilst the men were watering the horses, their womenfolk were busy in the cool barn, setting out the food they had brought with them. And everywhere I looked there were children, running madly about the place, and their mothers screaming at them not to soil their Sunday clothes. Little Lizzie's face was agog with excitement – she was not used to the company of children and was enthralled by their antics.

The preacher had not yet arrived, so it was decided to have the picnic first, as the children were hungry and thirsty after their hot dusty journey across the prairie. William helped me to the barn, my extra burden had caused my ankles to swell, and I felt most unsightly as I struggled to walk the short distance, but once inside the shade I was quickly found a seat and made much of by the women there. With a leg of prairie chicken in one hand and a glass of cool lemonade in the other, I felt most content, and very happy that my daughter was soon to be christened, and in such good company too.

William had hoisted Lizzie on to his shoulders, and I laughed at her gleeful expression as she tugged at his hair, and then in an instant, my laughter turned to a gasp of pain. I caught my breath for a second and then another stab came, the sheer agony of that spasm caused me to cry out in distress. The womenfolk knew instantly what was wrong, and Alice Murphy's eldest daughter quickly bundled the children outside to play, whilst Mary McDonald and Alice lifted me from the floor, and then between them manoeuvred me across the yard and into the cabin. William was on the porch within minutes, but was sharply told by the women to leave it to them. He'd done his work they said, and now it was his wife's turn.

I lay on the cot, taking deep breaths between the rapid pains that were so fierce I thought I'd be torn apart. This was totally unlike Lizzie's birthing. I had been expecting the same rhythm of contractions that I'd endured with her, but this one obviously considered a few painful twinges and a quick stab in the back quite sufficient, and with a final unexpected lunge he rushed into the world, yelling as soon as he saw the light.

"A fine boy," Mary said, as she placed him in my arms. I immediately burst into tears – some of joy, and some of relief. I had been so afraid of this confinement, frightened of my courage failing if the labour was long, but most of all the fear of being alone, with no female at my side. Good fortune as it was, I'd had the whole of Blue River's womanhood at my door that day.

William and Lizzie came in to see the babe, and I felt warmed by the look of gratitude that William gave me. Although he dearly loved his lovely daughter, I knew that secretly he'd hoped this second time for a son.

With such an easy birth I was not even tired, and lay propped up by pillows as the neighbours crowded into the cabin to offer their congratulations. I happily greeted everyone, feeling abundantly blessed, with my husband and children by my side.

The preacher's arrived, someone said. I smiled. His coming late was fortuitous: he would now *christen* both my children after all.

Blue River. 29th of March 1897.

A Prairie Harvest Festival

We had such merriment yesterday, and well into the night, that in fact we didn't reach our beds at all. We were celebrating, having had a bumper crop, and with the good prices it had raised we could pay our debts, and still leave enough to buy much needed household goods and perhaps a little treat for the children at Christmas time. Last year's bad harvest had almost finished us, and without William hiring out his labour we would have been in a sorry state.

We decided to give a party, and I, remembering the harvest suppers back home, suggested we have a proper English harvest festival. I wanted Lizzie and little Tom to know what fun they were, and to also revive my own happy memories. Back home they were the culmination of a year's hard work, and were looked forward to by everyone on the farm. For days ahead we would scour the woods for wild flowers to decorate the small village church, and the evening before the harvest service we would go from cottage to cottage asking for fruit and vegetables to put at the altar. We were never refused: even the poorest home would dig up a few potatoes or take a bunch of onions down from the outhouse where they were drying.

My mother would have been busy for at least a week before, baking hams and pies in preparation for the harvest supper, and the morning of the festival she would rise at dawn to bake special harvest bread. I always loved to watch her skilfully shape the risen dough into sheaves of corn, and cover them in beaten egg to give their golden colour when baked in the big oven by the range. The kitchen was cleared and long trestle tables set up, as we could have fifty or more at the supper. The farm labourers, their wives and children came, and my father always invited the old people, some of whom had worked for his own father. The children, if the weather was fine, sat out in the yard with their own table.

But first we would go to church for the harvest service, where we gave thanks for the good plentiful food we had harvested that year. And then everyone made their way back to the farms to enjoy their harvest suppers. For this special occasion my father would supply a barrel of home-brewed beer. He was not a drinking man himself but he recognised that his men had earned it. As the evening wore on some of the men who had over-indulged would sing old songs and even try to dance a jig. Such happy recollections, and I was quite determined to recapture them here on the prairie.

We didn't have a church to decorate or a vicar to take a service, but we could still have our own thanksgiving and a harvest supper. The invitation was verbally passed around and we expected most of the neighbourhood to come. I took the children out to gather flowers, or in little Tom's case a few colourful weeds, with which we decorated the barn. I prepared mounds of cold potato salad and side dishes of pickled cucumbers, and knowing that the womenfolk would not come empty handed I limited my baking to making bread rolls, and trying my hand at the sheaves of com bread that my mother was so competent at. I was not displeased at the result, although some had baked slightly misshapen.

Lizzie and I made corn dollies to give to the visiting children, and in fact the planning and anticipation was gratifying in itself. The morning of the party was fortunately bright and sunny, the sort of balmy day you often got in the fall. William had laid out planks on top of the hay bales to make supper tables, with further bales for seats. I put my bread out on the planks and decorated them with ears of com. I was feeling excited and almost as giddy as a young girl. William accused me in jest of having been at his whiskey still.

The first wagon to arrive was loaded to its limit with the O'Leary family who had travelled the furthest, having left home soon after daybreak. On their way they had picked up two other families, and their wagon seemed overflowing with passengers. It was not the normal country conveyance as Ray O'Leary had made it himself. It consisted of three tree trunks, each sawed into two lengthways, and these were fastened on to a six-wheel chassis, which was pulled by a team of horses, giving I should imagine a most uncomfortable journey. Their arrival with so many people clinging perilously to the timber made me think of Sunday school outings, when children were similarly piled into horse drawn charabancs.

Soon they were joined by other more conventional wagons, and I began to fret that there wouldn't be enough food to go round, but it was a foolish worry because, as always, loads of food had accompanied the guests. The planks were soon buckling with the weight of it, loaded down with hams, venison, and sweet potato pies, and a wide variety of salad dishes, all accompanied by my pickles and sour cheeses. Before we ate William said a prayer of thankfulness for the good harvest we had all been granted, and everyone, despite their own beliefs, said a heartily amen to it.

When all had eaten their fill, the planks were dismantled and the barn floor cleared for children's games, and later when the little ones were laid down to sleep in the wagons the music started up for dancing. The O'Leary's were a musical family, and always an asset at any party, as between them they had two fiddlers, an accordion player and a flutist. A rare mixture, but no one found it strange, as we were happy to dance whatever the tune.

The laughter and merrymaking went on until the early hours, when, fortified by soup and com bread, the weary but happy neighbours headed off down the track. Everyone had enjoyed our Canadian harvest festival, and I would write my mother to tell her all about it. The following day little Lizzie had asked if we could have another one, and I said yes if, God willing, we had a good harvest next year.

Blue River, 20th of September 1898.

The Travelling Man

The Travelling Man was always a welcome sight when he appeared at the isolated Blue River homesteads, a familiar figure riding down the track, leading his packhorse alongside. Children's faces lit up at the sight of him, knowing that amongst his goods there would be sweets and small toys. As well as the stock he carried with him, it was also a chance to look through his catalogues, and place an order for such diverse articles as ladies corsets, men's working dungarees or new farming appliances. These would be delivered later by a carter to the trading post, usually a few months later, depending on the Travelling Man's route.

There were so many things I would like to order, but money was always scarce, which was the reason William had to keep working on the rail road. I hated the long periods he was away, but it was a necessity as we were hardly making a living from the farm. The small orders I was able to give were always for essential items, although I would buy a few sweets for the children, not being able to resist their pleading looks.

The purchase I most longed to make was a complete set of Charles Dickens. I had found his works in the book catalogue and really hungered to possess them, but the price was high, and I knew that they would never be within my means. I had tried to save a few cents to put by in the hope that one day I could order them, but there was always another call on my meagre savings, if not winter boots for the children, it would be new tools that William needed.

Books were the one thing I missed most from home. I'd always been a prolific reader; my family used to make fun of me for having my head buried in a book whenever I could. My father despite his farming background was quite a scholar, and the house was full of literature. Contrary to normal country practice, he had kept my siblings and I at school until our sixteenth birthdays. I think he'd cherished hopes that I would become a teacher like my mother had been, and I must have spoilt this ambition when I left for Canada to marry William.

Now a parent myself I realised his good intentions were entirely on my behalf. I worried that, isolated as we were, my children would not get the benefits of the good education that I had been lucky enough to receive. I had already taught Lizzie to read, and little Tom was beginning to form his letters too, but I would have liked books in the house to further feed their minds. And I freely admit to feed mine as well.

Sometimes I despaired of ever having a conversation that was not connected with children, recipes or household needs. William was not of a bookish mind and had never felt the lack of them, and my neighbours, whilst being generally the kindest of souls, had not my taste for the written word.

Despite my lack of money I looked forward to the Travelling Man's visits, he brought with him a flavour of city life, and talked of politics and the musical evenings he attended when in Montreal. I had no jealousy of his urban life, I loved the prairies, but it was nice to talk of more cultural things. I would give him coffee and cake, and listen to his stories. William would come in from the yard and place his few orders before leaving me to enjoy the company of my well-read companion.

William was working away the next time he called, and in his bag he had the Dickens books that I had so longed for. He put them in my hands, and as I stroked their beautiful leather covers I could smell the newness of their print, and it was like no other aroma I had ever known before.

I reluctantly handed them back, explaining I still couldn't afford them and didn't expect to in the future. I told him that I was sorry he had taken up so much space in his travel bags in hope of a sale. He told me that there were other paths I could take to have ownership of them, but I quickly assured him that William and I would not take credit, having no desire for debts we could never pay.

He took a coloured bouncy ball out of his bag and gave it to the children telling them to see how well it would bounce against the barn door. They excitedly ran outside to test its power. And in my innocence I thought how kind he was, that is until I found myself being pushed against the bed, and held in a tight grip whilst he kissed and fumbled me. I was so shocked it took a minute before I struggled free, and retaliated by kicking him hard in the groin. I had obviously found my target as he groaned and crawled to the door, making as hasty an exit that his pain would allow.

I was horrified by what he had tried to do, and was angered by my own naivety, and my unconcealed desire for the books, which had made him think I would accept his lovemaking in exchange for his gift of them. I felt smirched by his behaviour, and went out onto the porch to tell him so, and to demand that he never show his face in Blue River again as I couldn't guarantee his safety. He painfully mounted his horse and rode off down the track, I felt some satisfaction in the knowledge that he would have an uncomfortable ride home.

His absence was not noticed until the following spring, and as a result the trading post acquired some catalogues, and the Travelling Man was no longer needed. I didn't tell William or anyone else about my ordeal, ashamed that my gullibility had led to such an incident.

The only beneficiaries of the tawdry episode were the children: they loved their bouncy ball that the nice man had given them.

Blue River. 10th of October 1898.

A Sudden Storm

I stared fixedly at the clock as each new spasm of pain engulfed me, the fierce contractions getting closer and sharper. I gritted my teeth, trying not to scream out loud, not wanting to wake the two children asleep in the next room. It was over an hour since William had left, driving off into the night heading for the McDonald's place. It was all of ten miles, but by leaving the trail and heading across country he could halve the journey. An early summer storm was blowing up as he left, and I prayed it wouldn't delay him. Another fierce pain overcame me and I gripped the table edge until it had passed, and then looked at the clock again, he should be here soon – please God.

Mary McDonald had promised to be here for my confinement, planning to arrive a few days before my due date, and staying on until I was on my feet again. I'd done a similar service for her, and she twice before for me. This coming one had been difficult from the start, laying me low for months with sickness just when William had needed my help with the harvesting, and kicking violently whenever I laid down to rest, and now, wilful to the end, had chosen its own inconvenient time to join us.

I'd been working on the land all day, picking stones whilst William raked behind me, little Lizzie following down the furrows with her own pail, and young Tom tied to a stake to stop him wandering whilst we worked. A sudden sharp pain in my back had stopped me in my tracks. I'd straightened up, wiped the sweat off my face, and waited for the pain to go. William had halted his raking and ran up to me looking anxious. "I'm alright," I'd said, and had gone back to my stone picking, but I wasn't – the nagging pain had not gone away.

Dusk comes quickly on the prairies, and I'd taken the children back to the cabin whilst William fed the stock and fastened up the horses for the night. With a good broth already simmering on the stove, and my bread put to rise, I was able to sit awhile, hoping the dull ache would lessen if I rested. William came in, soaked to the skin from a sudden downpour, and fighting to close the door against a strong wind that was gathering power as it raged across the open prairie. Seeing my tiredness he'd trimmed the lamp for me, and sent Lizzie to wash and undress Tom. I'd managed to serve supper and see the children to bed, and it was as I stood at the door to say goodnight that the first sharp contraction had hit me, I'd gasped and clung to the dresser for support. I'd known then that it was not simply tiredness, it was my impatient baby on its way, two weeks early, and me without a woman in the house.

"William," I'd quietly said, "go fetch Mary. I'm going to need her tonight." He'd glanced at my face which was taut with pain, and then quickly put on his boots again, held me close for a second, bid the children be good, and went out into the storm to harness the horses. I'd stood on the windswept porch until I could no longer hear the wagon wheels, or the steady gait of the horses as they sped across the familiar tracks. Another stab of pain, but mercifully brief, and I held my breath until it had passed. My eyes, growing used to the darkness, marvelled at the beauty of the storm clouds that scurried across the prairie skies. They entranced me with their savage intensity – the vast wild blackness that surrounded me held no fears, the ever changing face of this vast country had always held me in its thrall.

I went back indoors, fighting against the wind to close the cabin door, and once inside made preparations for my coming labour. I placed old newspapers on the bed, tore a ragged cotton sheet into strips, and tied two long ones to the bedpost ready for me to pull on if the birthing pains became unbearable. I filled pans and a large kettle with water and put them to boil on the range, and finally laid out Tom's old baby clothes and my best clean nightgown ready for my lying in. Satisfied that all was ready, I'd sat down to rest, allowing the pain to come and contemplating a long night's toil ahead.

And as I sat, my hands resting on this impatient babe who was far too eager to come, I begged it to wait awhile, at least until I had Mary by my side. I closed my eyes and must have dozed awhile, until a sharp pain seared through my body forcing me upright with the agony of it. I could hear the wind getting stronger, and the barn door banging with every gust – in his haste William must have left it open. Placing an old shawl around my shoulders I forced my way out through the cabin door. Heavy rain was now sweeping across the porch and caused me to slip, and tumble down the steps to the sodden earth, where I lay, weeping with pain and frustration.

I have no recollection of how long it was before an agonizing contraction forced me to my knees, and then upright as I clutched at the fearsome demon that had seemingly taken hold of my body. I screamed freely knowing that the noise of the wind would prevent the sleeping children hearing me. I trudged across the muddy yard still stubbornly intent on closing the barn door, and with the pains coming faster, with wet clothes and hair plastered to my body, and the screams ringing in my ears, I felt at one with the howling wind, and my cries just part of the storm's rising frenzy.

42

With each new wave of pain I fell to the floor, kneading the sodden soil with my hands, as if to bury the intensity of the forceful labour, and as I knelt I felt the sudden rush of warmth between my legs as my waters broke. My dragging saturated skirt was bunched up around the waist, my knees scratched and bleeding. I sat back on my heels, with face upturned to the rain, and I cursed, firstly William for making me pregnant, Mary McDonald for not being there as she'd promised, and thirdly William again for not closing the barn door. Another sharp stab of pain, and now my anger had turned to fear, and I silently prayed that I could make it to shelter – please God let this baby wait a little longer. I crawled the few yards needed to reach the barn, and then with a sharp intake of breath waited out the next contraction before making the final lunge inside. Once undercover I stopped and rested against a bale of hay, sobbing with relief and exhaustion, the pain now secondary to my fears. A sudden flash of lightening illuminated the barn, and in that brief moment I saw the sympathetic eyes of our milking cow looking down at me. William must have brought her in out of the storm. It was not that long ago that we had delivered her calf in this same spot, but at least she'd had both William and I in attendance, she had not been alone as I was.

More excruciating pain, this time so bad that I screamed until my parched hoarse voice could utter no more sound, sweat was dripping down my face, the salty liquid moisturising my parched lips. I was so afraid now, and so alone, I called out for my mother, never had I been so much in need of her. And where was William, he'd been gone such a long time, he must come soon – a terrifying crash of thunder shook the barn, and another convulsive shudder racked my body, I felt possessed by a monster and prayed for it all to end. My knees were drawn up to my chin as I waited for the next rush of pain, it soon came, and with it a desperate need to push. I was panting with exertion and whimpering with fear, but instinctively kept on pushing, and then in a miracle of release my son was born. He yelled out a strong lusty cry, I gathered him to me, overwhelmed with love and relief, and cried with him.

At that moment I heard the rattling of the wagon as it raced down the track, and soon the barn was lit by William's storm lantern as he and Mary McDonald stood at the door, gazing in amazement at my son and me.

Blue River. 2nd of June 1899.

The Prairie Bug

It had been another day of heavy rain, and the children fretful, having been cooped up in the cabin since early morning. Even little Tom had tried my patience, and he normally such a placid, happy child – he'd whined and hung around my skirts, driving me to distraction. Lizzie had tried to amuse him whilst I attended to the chores, but he had whimpered and pushed her away. Lizzie too was looking flushed and not quite her usual self. It had rained all week, and as much as the land needed refreshment I prayed it would soon cease – I had piles of wet washing to dry and a growing list of outside tasks that needed my attention. William was not due back until the weekend; he'd been gone over a month, working with a rail gang some hundred miles up country. The farm was neglected, but we sorely needed the money he would earn.

We had been lonely without him, and had seen no other human face other than James McDonald, who had called a fortnight since. He'd brought back the tools he'd borrowed, and also a side of bacon from the pig killing they'd had. The days had been long, and the sleepless nights with baby William had taken a toll of my normal good health and vitality. I felt low in spirits and short of temper, so when Lizzie complained of feeling poorly just as I'd sat down to rest, I was sharp with her, and sent her back to bed.

I must have snoozed for a while, and woke to the sound of her softly moaning. I rushed to her side and found her red of face and burning hot, her cotton night shirt soaked with sweat, her eyes glazed and holding no recognition. Little Tom slept peacefully by her side unaware, and undisturbed by her sudden affliction. I carried her to my bed, stripped her sweating body, and sponged her with cold water – she lay still and limp, her laboured breathing filling me with anxiety. I renewed my efforts, soaking a rag in the cooler waters of the outside rain tub and placing it on her brow. I flung the window open and wafted my apron to create a breeze, but she didn't respond. I felt angry at my lack of medical knowledge, and my inability to help her. I could see that she was slipping away, and frantic with fear, I took her in my arms and simply willed her to live, telling her repeatedly how much she was loved, and how precious she was to us – she stirred and seemed to smile, and then with a sudden choking noise in her throat she left me.

I sat rocking her lifeless body for the remainder of the night, my heart full of anguish and despair. With the first light of dawn I laid her on my bed, wrapping her gently in the white silk shawl that I'd worn on my wedding day – she had always admired it and I had promised her that she would wear it on hers. Mercifully, the next few hours seemed to pass in a blurred unawareness. I fed baby William whom I had left grumbling in his crib far too long for his comfort, and then taking William's heavy spade went out into the clearing at the back of the cabin and dug Lizzie's grave. I lined it with the goose feathered eiderdown that I'd brought out from England. It filled the hole with its soft downy warmth; I couldn't stand the thought of her being cold. I carried her out and gently laid her in the grave, and then ran back into the cabin for her beloved rag doll which I placed in her arms. Kneeling down on the damp soil I said a final farewell to my precious daughter, kissing her lips, and pushing a stray curl away from her eyes, and then wrapped the eiderdown tightly around her, promising my eternal love, and an everlasting memory.

I could hear little Tom calling me from the cabin, so I quickly piled the soil on top of her, and collected stones to cover the broken earth; I didn't want any animal to find her. After it was covered to my satisfaction I went back inside, lifted the crying baby from his crib and called out to little Tom that I was coming.

He was still in bed, flushed and crabby and asking for Lizzie. I held him tight and with a tremble in my voice told him she had gone to be an angel. He asked me if he could go with her and be one too. I placed the baby in his care and fled into the scullery where my choking sobs could break free.

I had no time or inclination to indulge my grief, as little Tom's fever had increased as the day progressed. He too flushed scarlet, and his body turned clammy with sweat, he cried for me if I left his side to attend to baby William, and I was torn apart between the two. As with Lizzie, I sponged him down and tried to get some liquid through his parched lips, but to no avail. How I wished my mother here, with her herbs and potions, she would have known how to cool him, or even one of the neighbours who might have advised me, or taken the crying baby off my hands whilst I tended my poor sick boy. He seemed to worsen as the day wore on, his hands were limp in mine, and his head lolled against my arms. I prayed so hard for his recovery, and when he seemed to rouse a little I thought my prayer answered.

Little Tom died whilst I was out in the yard drawing fresh water from the well. At long last the rain had stopped and a watery sun was shining, and I ran back into the cabin hopeful that he too was feeling better. At first I didn't realise that he had gone. I lifted up his head to coax him to take a drink, but he flopped back, his eyes staring blankly as I shook him desperately, trying to find some life. It was then that I lost my reason. I screamed until my voice was hoarse, and gave myself injury by beating my hands about my head. I cursed this wicked fever that had robbed me of two of my precious children, and hurled abuse at an absent husband who had not been there when most needed, and for good measure berated the very prairie which had bred this wretched bug.

Later, when some reason had returned, I washed little Tom's body. He looked peaceful with the coolness I'd been unable to achieve. I dressed him in a clean night shirt and gently brushed his damp hair, curling it round my fingers, imagining him just asleep and soon to awake, giving me one of the sweet smiles that made him look so like his father. I held him close in my arms trying to infuse some of my own vigour into his lifeless body. At last, accepting his loss, I kissed his cold lips, and wrapped him in one of my best linen sheets before carrying him outside to place his little body alongside Lizzie, in a grave I had dug earlier in the full frenzy of my grief.

As I went back into the cabin I saw my reflection in the scullery window, I looked like a mad woman, my hair hanging loose and wild, a deranged look in my eyes. I knew at that moment that I would never feel young again. Baby William was crying; I lifted him from his crib and pressed him tightly to my breast, and as nightfall came I took him into my bed. He refused to feed, and felt over warm to my touch. I too felt light headed, and a little flushed, so I placed the fretful baby close to my heart and then turned my face to the wall.

William found us there two days later on his return from the railroad, baby William still tight within my arms, but long gone to join his sister and brother. I was delirious with fever and grief and have no memory of that day. When I reluctantly returned to my senses I found Mary McDonald at my side, the room sweet-smelling, and my bed linen clean. I felt very weak, and in much denial of my loss. Lifting my head I searched for the crib and asked where my baby was. Mary took my hand and gently told me that my children had gone to a better place, where God would take good care of them. "No," I screamed, "I want them back."

Each day with her good care I improved in health, if not in spirit. I learnt that the sweating sickness had taken many lives, and other prairie homes shared our grief.

I found it difficult to meet William's eyes when he came each evening to sit by my side. I could feel his pain, but had no comfort to share. One such evening, he carried me from my bed out to the clearing at the back of the cabin, and showed me the three little graves lying side by side. He'd carved each a wooden cross, and had scattered wild flowers around them. It was distressing for me to see, but I gained some solace from knowing that they lay together, and that their graves were marked.

Soon Mary was needed back in her own home, her family looking for her return. She wanted me to go back with her for a visit, but kind as she was I refused. I needed time by myself, time to accept my loss. Every night I sat on the porch, searching for my little ones amongst the brightly shining stars. William left me alone, finding his own comfort elsewhere.

A few weeks later a kindly neighbour sent a travelling priest to bless the graves; he said a prayer and afterwards told me that God must have wanted them for his own. "What God," I scoffed, "what kind of God would snatch my innocent babies from me," and then I turned, and walked away.

Blue River. 3rd of August 1899.

Letters from Home

After our great loss I have neglected my journal, having no heart or desire to write of day to day matters, my pain too acute. Correspondence with my family in England also seemed irrelevant, and yet that has always been a crucial part of my life. I have always eagerly anticipated our trips to the trading post: more important than the change of scenery was the possibility of letters from home. The journey there would seem endless. I'd sit at William's side mentally urging the horses on to a greater speed – such was my need to have news of my dear ones back home.

On our arrival my impatience would not allow me to wait whilst William tethered the horses. I would take an unladylike leap from the wagon, and, lifting up my skirts, race inside the store. Eddie Wilks, the proprietor, would reach inside the mail box and search for our letters; he was so slow and fumbling, I wanted to snatch the box from his hand and tip them all out to make his task easier. At last he would hand me a bundle of mail and I would rush outside to sit on the store steps and sort through it. Discarding circulars and seed catalogues I would feverishly look for the envelopes that had an English stamp, and if none were found my disappointment would be excessive.

Sometimes months would pass without any news, and our journey back home would be dismal, with William feeling sad for me, and also depressed at his own lack of family correspondence. But if letters had come my joy was overwhelming, and I would hold the packages close to my heart. Just seeing my mother's familiar neat handwriting, or my sister's untidy scrawl, was magical, like quenching a raging thirst after weeks of drought. Our purchases made, I would sit quietly on the wagon whilst William loaded it, all the while holding the unopened letters on my lap, hoarding the opening of them until I had savoured the full joy of their arrival.

I would read, and re-read every letter until the ink had faded or was smudged by my ready tears. My mother's always told of her daily activities, and such were her descriptive powers I could almost feel myself back there with her. She would write that the hens had stopped laying, and of the problems she was having with a flighty dairy maid, and her annoyance that the strawberry jam she was making had not set properly. Cherishing every word, I could imagine her trim figure as she sat at the walnut bureau in the parlour, writing her letter and thinking of me. How I miss her.

Sometimes in the winter mail was delayed, and letters would accumulate to arrive months later, such as the day I received three all at once from Lucy, my younger sister. The first was full of her excitement at having been bridesmaid at our elder sister's wedding, a good six months past, and full of enthusiasm about the happy day. She had pressed me a rose from the bridal bouquet that had been picked from our own garden; I held it to my nose and thought I could still detect a faint aroma of that summer's day.

The second letter written a few months later excitedly informed me that I would soon share her own excitement of becoming an aunt, as Matilda, our newly married sister, was expecting a baby. She said that the whole family were overjoyed at the news, and already mother was knitting madly for the new babe. I realised that they had not yet received my last letter telling of my own pregnancy. How I wished I had my mother to knit and care for me.

Her third letter when I took it from the envelope was edged in black. I trembled, and placed it face down, greatly feared to read it, and sat awhile before finding the courage to take it up again. The news was bad: my elder sister was dead – she had suffered a miscarriage, and had bled to death. I clutched myself with grief; two months she had been dead, and I had gone about my business, quite unaware, and even joyful at my own happy news. And now I was filled with fear about my own condition, if she could die whilst ministered by my mother, and the village doctor, how would I survive?

William was downcast too, having received his own black edged letter: his beloved grandma had passed away. He had been granny reared and keenly felt his loss. The usual elation at having news of home was now tempered by our great sadness.

In that one mail collection I had been given news of my sister's wedding, her pregnancy, and then her funeral. We were both subdued, and had felt the measure of the distance that separated us from our loved ones.

Many weeks later a parcel of baby clothes arrived from my mother, six beautifully sewn nightgowns, and four knitted matinee coats that were all surely intended for Matilda's babe. I wondered how many tears had been shed over the packing of them, and I prayed that my baby would be strong and healthy enough to wear them.

Over the years we received other black edged letters, but none so distressing as the one that informed me of my father's death. I was shocked to think of him gone. In my mind he was still busy on the farm, or as I remembered him last, raising his hand to me when my ship departed from the Liverpool docks as I set off for Canada. My brother Arnold wrote to say that our mother was devastated, and sick at heart. Our father had died of a sudden heart failure as he and my brother were leading the horses and plough up to the top field. It had been quick and merciful, and he'd breathed his last in my brother's arms. I was distraught and my tears had no end. William had feared for the child I was carrying at the time, such was my grief.

Not all our letters were so grim. My sister was a faithful correspondent and would write with news of my old friends, or of any tasty village gossip that she thought might interest me. And my mother, now a widow and moved to a cottage down the lane, would always keep me in touch with the seasons – describing the beauty of the autumn leaves, or the splendour of an orchard tree weighed down with its crop of red apples, and the excitement of hearing the first cuckoo of the year. My mother was a real country woman, and took great pleasure in these things. She also grumbled a little about my brother's wife, who was now mistress of the farm, and according to my mother, very slovenly in her ways. It must have been hard for her to leave the home she had gone to on her marriage forty years earlier, and how I wished I could have been there to comfort her. These little snippets of news helped me feel that I was still part of the family, and brought them all closer.

This regular exchange of letters was to be a lifeline in the early days of my arrival in Canada. They helped keep my sanity when at first the sheer loneliness and the size and grandeur of my surroundings had threatened to engulf me. A few words of wisdom from my mother, and her chatty accounts of daily life back home, all played a part in my eventual acceptance of living in a log cabin on the prairie.

The only time I have ceased to correspond is this present bleak period whilst I mourn my precious children, when for months I have struggled through a blackness of spirit that I feel will never leave me. My mother must have sensed some tragedy, her recent letter implored me to write and tell her all was well. And so William eventually sent his own black edged letter to inform our families of the grievous blow we had suffered.

I have no strength or inclination at this time to ever write again.

Blue River, 1st of December 1899.

50

Going Home

I sat stiff and upright on the wagon seat, waiting for William to take the reins in his hands, and for us to start the first stage of our long journey. I sensed him looking at me, but my eyes remained focused on the track which stretched for miles ahead. A biting cold wind was sweeping across the open land, the first sign of approaching winter, but I neither shivered nor felt its force – I had no normal feelings anymore, I felt no emotion, just an emptiness inside of me, almost as if my heart had turned to stone.

As we reached the farm gate I suddenly demanded William to stop, and leaping from the wagon picked up my skirts, and ran like a wild thing until I reached the small windswept clearing that lay behind the cabin, where I fell to the ground and knelt alongside the three small mounds that were there. I embraced each one in turn, my tears saturating the crumbling soil. I caressed each of the little wooden crosses that William had so lovingly carved, and my grief knew no bounds.

I wanted to reach under the cold earth, and lie there with my babies and warm them against my aching breast. I was digging crazily with my bare hands when William came; he lifted me from the ground, stilling my trembling body with his. He too was weeping, but he gently took the silver locket from around my neck, opened it, and placed a few grains of soil from each little grave, to lie alongside the precious images of our children that it already contained. He then pressed it firmly into my hand, closing my fingers tightly over it. "Wear it next to your heart," he whispered, "and then you will always have a part of them with you." He led me back to the wagon, took up the reins and once more headed the horses through the gate and out onto the track. Within the hour we had crossed the boundary and left our land behind – neither of us looking back.

As we journeyed the only sound was the pounding of the horses' hooves on the grassy trail that we followed, we were both deep into our own private thoughts. As the miles between us and the farm lengthened I started to feel a sense of peace. I no longer would stand at the kitchen window staring at my children's graves, haunted always by the sounds of sweet Lizzie's laughter, and the vision of little Tom, playing happily outside with his lead soldiers, spending hours lining them up for battle and then carelessly pushing them over when called in for bed. I could still feel the tightness in my breast, and a sense of loss, without my cherished baby suckling against me.

The weight of my treasured locket, lying warm and close to my heart brought me great comfort. The graves, I reasoned, were just soil and stones, and the strong prairie winds would soon erase them, but my precious ones would always be with me wherever I went. The past months had been a dark and lonely time, the sudden sickness that had ravaged our little family had also left me deranged. At first I was angry that I had not gone with them, and had survived, but with such a grief that I threatened harm to myself. Now with the passing of time I was able to hide that outward anguish, but inwardly felt just a shell of that other person who had once been a mother. Whilst I was still in my madness kindly neighbours had come and packed away the children's clothes and toys. But occasionally I would come across something they had missed, a half-finished sampler that Lizzie had laboured on during the winter months, and I would suddenly see her little face all screwed up as she struggled to thread her needle, and I would quickly thrust it back into the drawer where I'd found it. Once, finding one of Tom's marbles was my undoing, so many times I had scolded him for leaving them underfoot, I held it close and wept bitter tears. Now these small mementoes were safely packed in the wicker basket that I held securely on my knee as we travelled.

During that dark and painful time I had gone about my daily chores as if in a trance. I'd baked, washed, scrubbed floors, and worked alongside William on the land. We'd sowed new seed, walking the long ploughed prairie together, but so alone. We lay alongside each other at night, weary but not sleeping, both as cold and distant as a block of winter ice. He too carried his grief tight inside him, afraid to let it loose. We rarely left the homestead, and after that first week of mourning our neighbours ceased to come by so often, not knowing what to say to us, and feeling guilty if they had their own healthy children in tow.

Summer had come late this year, bringing with it a searing heat that cracked open the soil, stunted wheat in its growth, and shrivelled the crops into the ground. A fine red dust had settled on the land, blown in by the warm prairie breezes. The very air I breathed seemed tainted and thick with a feverish humidity. Overcome by a sudden weariness of mind and body I'd sat out on the porch, staring bleakly at the shimmering distant horizon – it seemed to have no ending, as did my life. With a sudden urgency I'd left the cabin and gone in search of William. I found him sitting alone in the dimness of the barn, his hands idle, and a look of such sadness in his face that I reached out to him and held him close, and then for the first time we shared our grief, and wept together. Afterwards I raised my eyes to his and with new found strength implored him: "Take me home William, please take me home, I want to see my mother, and I need to feel English rain on my face, smell freshly mown grass, and to walk the country lanes again, please take me home."

And now just six weeks later that is what he's doing. The farm lease was quickly sold, our belongings distributed amongst the neighbourhood, and our goodbyes said, some partings hard, with friendship not given lightly on the prairies. We had many unspoken thoughts between us on the journey to Blue River Halt, both deep in painful recollections. It was only sixteen years ago that I had come out to join William. I smiled at the memories of that journey back to the farm, how happy we had been, halting the horses to kiss and cuddle, not caring how long it took to reach our destination because we had all the time in the world, our whole future stretching ahead of us. I had been so young and untested, so full of hope and anticipation, but now felt old and spiritless. I didn't want to allow my thoughts to trespass any further, too much pain lay there. William must have sensed my agitation because he glanced at me and took my hand in his.

As we neared the Halt I had sudden misgivings. Could I leave this country that I'd come to love, and whose very soil held all that was precious to me? But the pull of home was strong, and there was no going back. Arriving at the Halt we handed the horses and wagon to their waiting purchaser, who, anxious to be home before dark, sped off down the track, his own horse trotting behind. I could see that it had fretted William to watch them go, they had been faithful workers, and served him well. The train was not due for another hour or two, so we sat in the shade, our few belongings at our feet, both silent – there was nothing more to say.

The following morning I stood alone on the viewing platform at the rear of the train, watching the vast prairies slip by. I was still there as darkness fell. I felt sad to be leaving this magnificent country, and the wonderful people who were slowly taming it. My children had belonged here as I never could, and I was comforted to know that they would always be part of the earth that had been their birthright. In the dim light that remained I could see the terrain changing; we were approaching more wooded country with less open land. I took one last lingering look at my beloved prairie, and then, clutching my silver locket, went back inside.

The Pacific Queen on route to Montreal. 2nd of September 1900

More Tales from Grandma's Prairie Journal

Coming Back

As the train steamed its way across Canada I marvelled at my own daring, or as some back home had said, my foolishness. But I had been drawn back, as if some invisible cord had pulled me. And despite what well-wishers said, I knew it was not just the call of the three babes that I'd buried here; they were dear to my heart, and I was always aware that part of my very being was integrated deep in this country's soil. But it had been something more spiritual that had drawn me back, the strong feeling that although previously this land had tried and tested me, I'd still not yet had my fill of it.

It had been six years since I'd last rode this rail track. Then, it had been in the opposite direction when William and I had left for home. Our hearts had been weary and weighed down with grief, but even then I had never imagined or doubted that one day I would return. On this long journey westward I'd had ample time to recall and reflect on that time, and our life back in the old country.

It had been wonderful to feel my mother's arms around me, and to relish the comfort and love of my family again. It was healing to walk the tree-lined country lanes, and meet old friends, and comforting to pay my respects to my father and sister's graves that were already weathering in the village churchyard.

William had taken a labouring job with a local farmer. It was not to his liking, but a tied cottage in the village came with it so he had no choice. We were happy at first, and overjoyed when I became with child soon after moving in. Edward, whom I named after my father was born on a warm summer's evening nine months to the day that we'd arrived back home. It was an easy birth with my mother and sister in loving attendance, but later, when holding his little head to my breast I shed scalding tears onto his downy hair, as memories of my other sweet babes came flooding back. William too was very moved when he held him for the first time.

Within a year I was nursing another son, this one we called Thomas, named for William's father. I was content and happy, but occasionally I would yearn for the open spaces of the prairie, and think of the good neighbours we had left behind. Many times I would see a faraway look in William's green eyes and knew that he too was missing having his own land, and the freedom of his life in Canada.

We lost my dear mother the following year. She was very poorly at the end and had lost her reason. She cried out for my father to wipe his feet when he came in, and he long gone. I was grateful that I was there to comfort and nurse her. I still sorely miss her.

William was unhappy with his job, disliking the farmer he worked for. He'd become sullen and ill tempered, and we were no longer cordial with each other. He had taken to visiting the village inn after work, staying late, and seemingly finding a comfort there that he couldn't find at home. He would return late, stinking of ale, and looking to find conflict with me, which of course he did, my anger being quick to rise when I thought of the money he had wasted on drink whilst my children were going without shoes, and I was having to take charity from my brother's wife to feed and clothe them.

The old William whom I'd loved enough to leave home and family for had vanished. His handsome face was bloated and reddened by alcohol, and his previous gentle caring concern for me and the children was now brutal and abusive. Twice I left him, taking the children and fleeing to refuge with my sister, but each time he sobered up and came to fetch us back, begging me to give him another chance. In truth I no longer had love for him and went back out of pity. I thought many times of the early days on the prairie when we couldn't bear to be out of each other's sight, and despite the hardships we had laughed and loved together, and had been perfectly content with our destiny.

And then came that fateful mid-summer afternoon when he was brought back to the cottage, lying face down on a farm gate, his neck broken by the tumble he had taken whilst topping a newly built haystack. He'd been drinking from his bottle all day, but whilst the other workers had supped cold tea his had been full of beer, and that combined with the hot sun had given him a dizzy spell, causing him to lose his balance.

I shed no tears. This William that we laid to rest alongside his father was not my William, this was a stranger, a man who couldn't come to terms with the hardships of life, and had drank away his sorrow. I mourned in private the man he had been, the lover and dear friend whom I'd somehow lost.

The farmer gave us notice to quit the cottage within the week, so my brother took us in, and the boys and I shared my old bedroom up in the eaves of the farmhouse. My sister-in-law made it plain that this was not to her liking, she didn't relish having another woman about the place, although she adored my two sons and to my discomfort spoilt and made much of them. They soon had the run of the place and were happy following my brother around the farm, or in the kitchen being fed titbits by their aunt. I felt restless and despondent, with no defined role to play, and a sense of dissatisfaction with my life.

Thoughts of returning to Canada were constantly in my mind. I had kept up correspondence with many of my prairie friends and they constantly urged me to return. They said the province was prospering with a larger population, and with good prospects of employment; in fact, Mary McDonald had urged me to apply for the tenure of the newly built station house that the railroad had provided at Blue River Halt. My brother cautioned me against making hasty decisions, but I was never one to resist a challenge, and the very thought of returning to Canada had filled me with excitement and a renewed zest for life. Within weeks, with Mary's help, I had secured the tenancy of the station house and was making preparations to depart.

The only obstacle to my going was my two boys, both now settled on the farm, and Edward happy at the village school – they decidedly didn't want to go. On reflection I could see how disruptive it would be for them, having newly found a father figure in my brother, and an adoring aunt who loved them as her own. My brother suggested I leave them with him until I was settled and could offer them a stable home. My sister-in-law, who was childless, urged me to go and make a new life for myself, making it obvious that she was anxious to see the back of me, but desperate to keep the boys. I was torn apart by the choice I had to make, my love for my sons against an opportunity that I might never have again.

I sailed from Liverpool three weeks later, my eyes blinded by tears as I hugged and kissed my children's sweet faces as we said our goodbyes on the dockside. The evening before my departure I had visited the village churchyard and said farewell to my loved ones buried there. For the first time since his death I approached William's grave, and placed a spray of wild roses next to his simple wooden cross. I knelt down and scooped a little soil into my bag. "I will take it with me to Blue River," I whispered, "and throw it on the prairie for you, William." And then at last I wept for him.

The train shook a little as it passed over a bridge, its wheels rattling on the wooden slats. It roused me from my musing and I stood and walked through the carriages to the viewing platform at the rear where I was just in time to see the first light of dawn breaking on the horizon. Such was the magnificence and beauty of it that I caught my breath in awe, I'd forgotten how wonderful a prairie dawn could be. I wanted to reach out and embrace the whole landscape. I knew then that I had made the right choice in coming back, this great country was my future, and I hoped that one day my sons would join me and make it theirs too. But just for now I was happy to be back on my beloved prairies.

Travelling by railroad across Ontario. 10th of August 1906.

The Station House

"Blue River Halt, anyone for Blue River." The strident voice of the conductor echoed through the carriage as he made his way down the aisle. He went on to say that the train would be taking on fuel, and passengers could take advantage of the dining and wash up facilities that were available at the station house. I listened intently, knowing that I would be the provider of these amenities within the week – I hoped that my capabilities would be adequate.

I had mixed feelings about my imminent arrival: much excitement and anticipation, but both overlaid by the sudden surge of memories that the conductor's first announcement had awakened. My thoughts immediately went back to my previous arrival in Blue River, and I mourned the innocent, naive young girl that I had been. I recalled the long wait whilst sat on the lone wooden bench, fearful that William wouldn't come, and then my joy when at last he did. The train jerked to a standstill and I let my memories go. I was back where I wanted to be, older and wiser, but prepared to make a success of this second chance. With renewed resolution I straightened my hat, smoothed down my crumpled skirt, took up my bags and prepared to step off the train, and face whatever the future sent me.

I was taken by surprise to find myself on a firm wooden platform furnished with half a dozen benches and even a small booking office – what progress from my previous arrival, when I'd had to take my life in my hands and leap from the train to land on the rough cinder track. Nearby, a smart, newly painted sign proclaimed it to be Blue River Halt, population 820.

I was even more taken aback by my first view of the station house – it was a pleasing sight, a two storey white timbered building that fitted amongst the surrounding pine trees to perfection. Its front door opened on to the platform, and it was in that direction that the passengers from the train were making their way. I followed them into a large hallway which was signed to washrooms and dining room, the whole atmosphere being light and airy, and a welcome haven for weary travellers to partake of a hot meal, and to refresh themselves before re-boarding the train to continue their journey.

A middle aged woman bustled forward to greet me, and as I was the only passenger to embark with luggage she had assumed correctly that I was the expected new tenant. She bid me to sit awhile whilst she served up a mutton stew to the waiting passengers, and then she said she would make me welcome. Tired of sitting I wandered outside to explore any further changes. I hardly recognised the track that had led up to the Halt: before I had left it had just been an unmarked grassy trail, and now it was a paved street, lined either side with wooden cabins, each with their own patch of land. A corn and animal feed merchant had opened up a store, and opposite was stabling and a blacksmith's workshop. As William had always predicted the railroad had brought prosperity to the area. How I wished he could have seen for himself that his prophecy was coming true.

I could see the passengers going back to board the train so I returned to the station house to find the woman whom I had come to relieve. She was a kindly body who had been running the station house since it had opened twelve months earlier. She had recently lost her husband and wanted to move to Vancouver to be closer to her daughter, which was sad for her, but most fortunate for me, as it had given me this wonderful opportunity.

She hoped to catch the next train to Vancouver which was due within the week, so I had much to learn. Besides the dining room there were four letting rooms plus a bedroom and sitting room for my personal use. The revenue from the dining room and rentals would be mine, but in return I had to keep the station in good order, provide hot food for the rail passengers who so desired it, and to keep the wash room clean and tidy, and well supplied with soap and fresh towels. One of the bedrooms was for the use of the engine driver who would hand over the train to a waiting colleague and then have a rest period before taking it over again on its return journey.

I tried to acquire as much information as my mind could accept, but all too soon the week was up, the keys handed over, and I was cooking and serving thirty portions of steak and kidney pie to the passengers of the Vancouver bound train that my mentor was leaving on. Tired but happy, I waved her off and went back inside to survey the domain that was now all mine. The next morning I was up early to cook breakfast for the four lodgers I had inherited, and the overnight engine driver. I was eager to make the changes I had planned whilst following the previous tenant around. First on my list was a good spring clean of the whole house, as by my standards it was none too clean. Alongside my lodgers I'd also been bequeathed two members of staff, a married couple who lived in one of the cabins alongside the blacksmith's forge. Agnes and Rickie West had left the slums of Manchester thirty years earlier and travelled to Canada in search of a better life, but after years of struggle they had come to the conclusion that this was as good as it was going to get. Rickie was employed by the rail company to help refuel the engines and also work in the ticket office when required. He was a ferrety-faced little man whom I'd disliked on sight, his manner was both surly and arrogant, and I could find nothing agreeable about him at all. His wife Agnes had been employed as a cleaner by my predecessor, who had spoken highly of her; she was a nice little woman, but I had my doubts about her cleaning abilities, and the proof of her work was not encouraging. I decided not to be hasty and give her a chance to improve as she would not be easy to replace.

The following days were long and hard, but I'd started to get used to the railway timetable and learnt to adjust my hours to fit in with the trains' arrivals. Four times a week I cooked in readiness for the expected diners, never sure how many to expect, and occasionally having to skimp on portions. At other times I had food to spare when fewer passengers had left the train.

My four lodgers were all railway men, and would often be away repairing the track, perhaps fifty miles or more up country. So consequently my profits fluctuated from week to week, but I was managing to save a little, always with the aim of having enough money to bring my boys over.

In those first few weeks I had visits from all my old neighbours. I was touched that in the height of summer, when they could ill spare the time, they had taken the trouble to travel to the Halt to see me. Mary McDonald was the first to come, and we hugged and cried together until our blouses were quite damp with tears. She was stouter than I remembered, but still had the sweet wholesome face that had always been such a comfort to me. She said that once the planting was done she would hold a barn dance, and I could meet the newcomers who had become part of the community in my absence. It was painful to talk of William, but inevitable that they would. I was reticent to tell of his descent into alcoholism, and preferred his old friends to think of him as they had last seen him.

A few weeks later I went to the promised dance at the McDonald's place. Their eldest son kindly drove their wagon down to the Halt to fetch me. He was now a strapping sixteen year old young man, totally changed from the shy lad I remembered, he was now confident and eager to please. Because of the distance I had arranged for Agnes to stay over at the station house to allow me to spend the night with Mary. During the journey we passed the turning that had led to William's farm, and conversation dried up, as the young man also knew where the fork on the track led to. My heart desperately wanted him to turn the horses and take me there, but my head told me that with the prairie winds my three little graves would have been long scattered, and I didn't have the courage to view such damage.

I was made very welcome on our arrival, and soon became re-acquainted with many old neighbours and friends. No one spoke of William, either fearful of upsetting me, or having been well primed by Mary McDonald kept his name out of the conversation. The only person to mention his loss was Cissie Anderson, now long married to a Dutch farmer over at Buffalo Creek, and blessed with two healthy sons. By the look of her she had another one on the way. She held me close and whispered her sadness at the news of William's death. "He was a fine man," she said. I hugged her back, always knowing that she had loved him too.

I danced the night away, enjoying myself as if I was a young girl again. There was never a shortage of partners at a prairie dance – men always outnumbered the womenfolk, and I was quite dizzy and breathless with so much attention. Early next morning I made an early start when a young farmer who was heading for the blacksmith's drove me back to the station house, just in time for my lodgers' dinners.

Now that I had made social contacts with old and new Blue River friends I felt part of the community again, and very content to be back amongst them. All I needed to make my happiness complete was to have my two sons here with me. I made plans to write that very day to ask my brother to send them – I could wait no longer for their coming.

Station House, Blue River Halt. 18th of April 1907.

Old Sam

Old Sam seemed to have appeared out of thin air, although I suspected he had been riding illegally on a Vancouver bound goods train that had briefly stopped at Blue River Halt the previous evening, most likely by jumping off whilst it was being loaded with fuel.

The first I saw of him was early the next morning when I heard a commotion out on the platform, and on investigating found Rickie West manhandling a slight stooped figure who was loudly protesting at his rough treatment. Rickie said he'd found him asleep on the floor of the booking office, and as arrogant as ever demanded that I leave him to deal with the culprit, and all the while cuffing the unfortunate man about the head. Barely able to disguise my dislike of his domineering manner, I insisted that he stop the violence, and unhand the poor wretch.

Not used to being told what to do by a woman, he became aggressive, and continued to beat the unfortunate man. He had clearly underestimated me. I was not of the nature to back down when facing a bully, and turning I saw the yard brush propped against the wall, which when taken into my hands became a weapon. But like all bullies he had no stomach for confrontation and quickly let go of his victim, and stomped off the platform in a rage – I could only hope that he would not vent his feelings on poor Agnes.

The stooped figure straightened himself to his full height, which was at the most not quite five foot. He had a wizened little face of a definite eastern look, with tiny button eyes that were shrewdly looking me up and down. He was dressed in a grey cotton tunic top with matching trousers, over which he wore a battered leather jacket that almost reached to his feet. Deciding that he was far from menacing, I asked him if he was hungry, the least I could do after the battering he had taken from Rickie.

I made him some breakfast and asked where he was bound; he replied in a high squeaky voice that seemed to suit his frame, "Nowhere special missy, maybe I stay here, work for you missy." I was at a loss how to deal with his reply, and with his sad little eyes pleading didn't have the heart to send him on his way. So I had quite unexpectedly acquired a new member of staff.

In fact with time I realised that little Sam Lee was an accomplished actor, being able to adopt his sad little Chinese role whenever the occasion suited, and he soon dropped the accent and squeaky little voice after I'd said he could stay. But he was a good worker, and quickly made himself indispensable. He kept the platform immaculate, weeded the flower beds and could even turn his hand to cooking if necessary. He had no idea how old he was, although I estimated he was at least seventy years of age, and soon he became known to everyone as Old Sam.

At times I wished him far away as he followed me around like a lap dog, at first afraid to let me out of sight, although I believe this was on account of Rickie West who would glare aggressively every time he came across him. But within the year Rickie had run off with a buxom barmaid from the saloon, giving much relief to old Sam, and also to Agnes who was happily rid of a belligerent husband. We managed very well without him, which made me wonder what he had really done to earn his wage. The booking office and the refuelling were done competently by Old Sam, who combined his other duties with ease.

In time we got Old Sam's history; he would entertain us on a winter's night with tales of his youth, and I was never sure where the truth and fiction parted company. He had been born in the goldfields, the only child of a Chinese mother and a French father, parentage which explained his oriental looks and Gallic charm. His mother had cooked for the miners, and in Old Sam's words had obviously offered a little more than food to the Frenchman. When he was still a child she had married a Chinese man from whom his surname of Lee came. They had left the goldfields and moved to Montreal where they opened a diner catering for the seamen at the quayside. But Old Sam said his stepfather was brutal to him, and his mother powerless to intervene, so he stowed away on one of the visiting ships and never saw either of them again.

At fourteen years of age he had twice travelled the world, working first as a deckhand and later as a cabin boy. He had jumped ship when arriving back in Canada, but found no trace of the diner or anyone who had any knowledge of where the couple had gone. He had then joined a travelling circus, first as a handy man, and later with practice, became a tightrope walker. He travelled the length and breadth of Canada, performing in small towns or isolated areas where people would come for many miles to see the show. He had eventually married one of the lady clowns who was a dwarf, which I suppose made him for the first time in his life feel tall.

He had left the circus after his wife died in childbirth along with the baby. He said he could no longer put his heart into the act, and felt guilty about her death, as she'd had a breathing problem and should never have had a child. After this he got himself a wagon and horse and went west, selling patent medicines, and Chinese potions that he'd made himself. I could well imagine him stood on his wagon selling gullible farmers and townspeople his wares, his high pitched voice full of sincerity. I began to think our old Sam a bit of a rogue. He confirmed this by saying that his next venture had put him in gaol for six months. He didn't elaborate but suggested it had all been a big mistake on the judge's part.

After his release he'd gone across the border into America, where according to his stories he had an eventful career in Chicago working as a runner for a gangster's mob. As neither Agnes or I had any notion of what a runner did, we were not overly impressed, and he seemed disappointed at our lack of reaction to this obviously important role. But Old Sam would soon pass on to another tale; nothing crushed his enthusiasm for story-telling.

There seemed few occupations he had not tried at some time or other, having covered most of America and Canada in his travels. He seemed content to settle in at the Halt, and having progressed from sleeping in the booking office he now had one of the small cabins belonging to the railroad. As I had surmised on his arrival he had been hitching a ride on a goods train, planning only to stop off one night before continuing on to Vancouver. My unexpected intervention in his life when I rescued him from his tormentor had completely changed his plans. I felt a little overwhelmed by his devotion, but he was a good worker and a most entertaining individual.

Old Sam was a born survivor, and I felt some affinity to that trait too.

Station House. 3rd of July 1907.

A Family Reunion

At last I had enough money saved to have my boys come and join me. This had been my sole aim since arriving in Blue River Halt. It had been over a year since I'd tearfully hugged and kissed them before embarking on the ship to journey to Canada. I sorely missed them, and they were always in my thoughts. I kept their photographs on my dressing table, and every night touched their dear faces before retiring to bed, and in my every letter I promised that soon we would be together again. As time passed I became anxious that they might be forgetting me, and in truth I sometimes found it difficult to recall their faces, and often allowed their sweet ways to fade from my mind.

My brother was always punctual with his letters, never failing to keep me informed of the children's welfare and progress. I had worried for over two months after he had written to tell me that both had come down with the measles, waiting in suspense for his next missive to learn of their recovery.

Edward now wrote a clear hand of his own, and would pen me short accounts of his daily life. And little Thomas always sent pictures that he had specially drawn. I knew that they were happy and well cared for, but a mother's love can never be totally replaced, and I was sure that, like me, they were longing for the day we could be reunited.

I had been sparing with my own needs as every dollar saved was a step nearer to their coming. And now with this month's salary I had enough to purchase their tickets. A helpful train conductor had offered to purchase the shipping berths on his return home to Montreal, and he duly handed them to me on his next outward trip. He also kindly promised to arrange his duties, to enable him to chaperone them on their long rail journey to Blue River Halt after they had arrived in Canada. People were very kind and understood a mother's need to have her children with her.

The Halt's newly arrived doctor's wife had been a teacher in her youth, and said she would be happy to have them as pupils alongside the three children of Will and Bessie Ward, the proprietors of the recently opened dry goods store. This had solved a worrying problem, as I had thought I would have to tutor them myself.

With all the details arranged I sat down to write the letter that I had waited so long to send. Enclosing all the tickets I asked my brother if he would take the boys to Liverpool and see them safely aboard the ship, and if possible find a respectable woman who was also travelling to keep a charge of them, and I enclosed ten dollars for this purpose. I thanked him and my sister-in-law for the excellent care they had given to my sons and said I would be forever in their debt. I told them that I was not unaware of the loss that they would feel, but I was sure they would realise the pressing need I had to see my children again. I went on to ask if he would confirm by cable their embarkation date so that I could arrange their rail travel.

The next six weeks passed in a whirl of activity. I redecorated a spare bedroom and furnished it with a comfortable double bed. And old Sam, who was handy with a saw, made a bookcase and a deep pine chest for their toys. I spent many happy hours scouring the catalogues, choosing games and gifts, I knitted warm jumpers and sewed thick wool pants for them, reckoning their English clothes would not be suitable for the cold of the Canadian winter. I had a problem guessing their sizes, but measured the Ward children who were of a similar age. I believe on reflection that I must have driven Angie, and most of Blue River Halt, quite distracted with the constant talk of my coming children. I was by now counting the days before they were due to leave, and had great difficulty in containing my excitement.

At last the long awaited day arrived. I imagined the boys excitedly exploring the ship that was to bring them to me, and their possible tearful farewells to England. I realised what a wrench it would be for their uncle and aunt to part with them, but was sure that they would understand that it was better for the children to be with their mother. I waited patiently for old Ned who handled the telegraph office to come across with a cable, and twice went over to his office to enquire if it had come. By late afternoon my patience had run out and I once more crossed the road, but this time to send my own – *Why haven't you cabled? Are the boys on the boat? Please let me know.*

I spent an anxious night without rest or peace of mind, and when old Ned came with a return cable next morning I had already been through every possible illness or disasters that could have befallen them on their way to Liverpool. However the cable gave me no answers just a brief few words to say – *Boys not embarked, a letter on the way.*

I was by now quite distraught and had to be restrained from jumping on the next through train to Montreal. Angie prevailed on me to take a sleeping draught and to lie down for a while, and to my surprise I slept for the remainder of the day, waking much calmer and more prepared to consider the possible reasons for my brother's reply. Maybe one of the boys had come down with an infection, neither had yet had chickenpox or mumps, or perhaps my brother or his wife was ill. But surely someone could have taken them to Liverpool.

My mind was tortured for a further three weeks until at last the mail was delivered. I think everyone in Blue River Halt was as eagerly awaiting its arrival as I was. I tore open the envelope and scanned the closely written sheets it contained, noting an extra one in Edward's childish scrawl that I hastily read –

Dearest Mamma,

Thank you for sending the tickets. Don't be angry that we have not used them, but both Thomas and I want to stay in England with Uncle Ed and Aunt Nell. We like living on the farm, and Uncle Ed is going to buy us a pony at the next horse fair. We both have puppies from Rover's last litter, so you see Mamma we couldn't leave them, as they would pine for us. We like our school here and have lots of friends. Also Uncle Ed needs me – he says I'm his right hand man and couldn't manage without me. Thomas doesn't want to come because he's frightened of the grizzly bears that the Vicar told him live in Canada. So Mamma we are staying here, please write and tell Uncle Ed that you don't mind, because he's worried that you will be mad with him.

I will write again soon, and Thomas will too when he gets better with his letters.

Your loving son

Edward xx

Ps. Do be careful of the bears Mamma.

I laid the letter aside. I couldn't as yet read the bulky one from my brother; my eyes were too wet with tears, my throat too dry to speak. Agnes looked on in alarm as she watched me struggle to regain my composure, but was sensitive enough to see I needed to be alone.

Passengers from the train that had brought the mail needed to be fed so I splashed water on my face, tidied my hair and joined Agnes in the dining room. Later, alone in the parlour, I read my brother's letter. He was obviously concerned for my reaction, but underneath his troubled words I sensed his joy that my two sons wanted to stay with him. In short he promised to love them as his own, saying that naturally on his death the farm would be theirs, and that there would always be a home there for me too. His wife had added a postscript to say that she loved them as her own, but would never let them forget that I was their mother.

My instinct was to catch the next train through to Montreal and take a berth on the first available boat leaving for England, and once there I would collect my children and never let them out of my sight again.

Fortunately Mary McDonald came to the Halt the following day. Jim was collecting some tools he'd ordered and she'd seized the chance to spend a few hours at the Station House with me. There was no one I'd rather see; she was always to be relied on for comfort and sound advice. Expecting to see me blooming with elation at the thought of my boys coming, she was dismayed to find me so desolate. After reading the letters she took my hands in hers, and counselled me to do nothing rash. "Your boys are well and obviously happy, let them be," she said. "Think of what you are asking them to do, look at what you are offering here – no proper school, no friends, and the bit of spare time you have from your job is not enough to properly mother them." I knew that she was right, and that only a true friend could be so candid with the truth. I realised that I had lost my right to claim my children when I'd left them behind to follow my own dream in Canada. "You will see them again one day," promised Mary, "I'm quite sure they will come to find you."

I wrote back to the boys that night, telling them that although disappointed I understood their wish to stay in England. I said they could come to me whenever they so desired, but meantime bade them be good and mind their uncle and aunt, and remember me in their prayers. I added a postscript that I would be careful around the grizzly bears. To my brother I wrote only that he should care for them as he thought best, but to always tell them that their mother loved them dearly. As time passed, and in the privacy of my room, I would weep bitter tears at their loss. Despite my sore heart and the huge disappointment, I always remained positive that my destiny was here on the prairies.

The Station House. 5th of September 1909.

Meeting Mac

It was late fall when I first saw Mac. He came striding down the rail track, a rifle and saddle in his hands, and his wide shoulders bowed down with furs and pelts. From a distance he looked a wild fierce figure with six months growth of beard on his face, and a purposeful gait that bespoke no argument.

I was alone. Agnes was away visiting her daughter in Vancouver, old Sam had gone for supplies and would not be back before dark, and my three lodgers were working up country for a week or two. I fetched old Sam's hunting rifle, and quickly loaded it before going out onto the platform to await the stranger's arrival.

As he approached the station I stepped out of the shadows and ordered him to put down his rifle, and to stay exactly where he was, my steady hand pointing the gun directly at his head. Close up he looked even more disreputable, and despite the width of the platform between us I could smell the unpleasant aroma that he conveyed.

Showing no sign of alarm he slowly relinquished his heavy load, taking care not to damage the valuable furs as he piled them neatly on the ground, and then unhurriedly placed his rifle and saddle by their side. Having done my bidding he turned and flashed me a disarming grin, his white teeth reflecting oddly against the darkness of his skin and beard.

"Excuse me Ma'am," he said, "but can I ask you to lower that gun you seem set to blow my head off with? I would like to keep it a while longer as I'm mighty hungry." I felt a little foolish and lowered the gun slightly, but still kept my finger on the trigger, reasoning that even a rogue could have a charming smile.

He asked for some hot food, saying he had been walking the rail track all night, having lost his horse some twenty miles back; he'd had to shoot her after she'd stumbled and broken her leg. He seemed genuine, so I discarded my suspicions and put down the gun and agreed to cook him a meal, but suggested he might like to freshen up in the outhouse whilst I prepared it.

I sliced two big rashers of ham and fried them with half a dozen eggs. He wolfed them down, wiping his plate clean with a fresh baked loaf of bread. I fed him on the back porch, because despite my suggesting he clean up a little he was still smelling pretty bad, and I didn't want him in my dining room. He ate in silence, only pausing to drain his coffee cup. I fetched the pot from the kitchen and gave him a refill. When he'd finished he took a battered tin of tobacco from his pocket and filled his pipe, which when lit emitted such a vile odour that I was glad I'd not allowed him indoors.

As I cleared his empty plate away, I asked him where he had been heading for when his horse had so fatefully stumbled. He said he'd been making for the trading post, hoping to catch the fur agent before he left, this being the dealer's final visit before winter set in.

"Where's your man?" he suddenly asked.

"Not far away," I cautiously replied. In spite of his dazzling smile, and the brilliance of the blue eyes that were scrutinizing my face, and causing me to blush, I thought it prudent to claim a spouse who could be called upon if necessary. He said he needed a horse to transport his furs and pelts to the trading post and would my man sell him one. I gave him a searching look, knowing that for the past six months he would have been trapping in the wilderness, working towards this goal.

Appreciating his need I made a quick decision, telling him he could have the loan of our horse and wagon. I was surprised by my own gullibility, but I felt it a shame if he missed the agent. Trappers had been passing this way for a fortnight or more, so he would need to hurry if he was to find the agent still there. He flashed me that devastating smile again, and I saw a flash of a dimple on his hairy cheek. Feeling flustered I brusquely told him that he must return them straight away, or I would have the Mounties after him.

He quickly hitched the horses to the wagon, loaded up his furs, and with yet another of his overwhelming smiles and a doff of his shabby hat, he was off down the track. I stood on the back porch and watched until the wagon was lost in a screen of dust, and then turned and went indoors, wondering ruefully if I would ever see him, or my horses and wagon, again.

Old Sam arrived back early evening in quite a sweat, having seen the station wagon travelling at breakneck speed towards the trading post. He'd debated if to turn and follow it, or hasten back to the Halt to see if I was alright. I explained I'd loaned it to a stranger, which when put into words sounded rather lame, and Old Sam's troubled look re-enforced my own disquiet.

Two days later the wagon and horses were returned, driven by a lad from the trading post, his own horse following behind. In spite of my relief at their return I felt a sense of disappointment that the blue eyed trapper had not accompanied them. The lad said he had done well with his furs and pelts, and had purchased a horse and provisions before riding off on the Black Rock trail. "Probably drunk and shacked up with a tart by now," remarked Old Sam. "These trappers live for months like hermits, holed up in their shacks, and they go a little mad when they reach civilization again."

"Haven't you got work to do?" I tartly reminded him, not wanting to think about the smiling blue eyed trapper in some tart's arms.

I discreetly questioned the proprietor the next time I visited the trading post, asking him about the fur trade and the trappers. I suffered a half-hour tirade on the thieving prices they demanded before I bluntly asked him about the one who had arrived in the Halt's wagon. "You mean Mac, the half-breed," he said, looking at me knowingly beneath his bushy eyebrows. "All the ladies ask after him." I quickly paid him and flounced out of the store, my face burning, and my purchases not completed.

His assistant, Irish Ted, followed me out and helped load the wagon. He came up close and whispered, "I know your trapper well, known him since his father fetched him from the Cree camp when he was only knee high. Mac's his name; his dad was Jimmie McKenzie, a trapper who came from bonny Scotland. His mother was a full blood Cree, and they lived together out in the sticks, but she went back to the tribe to have the nipper, and she stayed there after he was born. Buck naked he was when I went with Jimmie to fetch him home after his mother's death, running around with the other Cree kids, and jabbering in their lingo too."

I stopped him there, and thanked him for the information, but said the trapper and his ancestry was of no possible interest to me. I then climbed onto the wagon, took up the reins and turned the horses for home. But as I followed the trail my thoughts were on the half-breed trapper, his smile, and the admiring look I had seen in his eyes when he'd first approached the platform, and the mocking way he had disarmed me. Such foolishness, I told myself, and urged the horses on; a train was due that night and I had bread yet to make.

Later that evening, as the Vancouver-bound train drew to a halt, the guard threw me a parcel. "Special delivery from Black Rock," he said. Occupied with feeding the dozen or more passengers who had alighted, I carelessly put it aside. It was only after the train had departed that I had chance to open it. I was puzzled: I had ordered nothing and had no acquaintance with anyone in Black Rock, but a sudden notion came to me, and my fingers trembled as I tore the paper open, and when a beautiful fox cape tumbled out I was quite overcome – in my whole life I had never before had anything so precious. I placed it around my shoulders, caressing its soft elegant perfection. There was no message included, but I didn't need one.

Two weeks later he came, as I'd known he would.

Station House, Blue River Halt. 15th of October 1909.

A New Lodger

When Mac finally came, he found me at my washtub, with steam rising all around me, and my shirt top damp as I struggled to squeeze the last of the water from a heavy sheet. I immediately sensed his presence but felt too embarrassed to turn and greet him – my face and hands were reddened from the heat of the copper fire, and my hair was wispy and curling around my face. My heart was racing fit to burst, and I wanted the ground to open up and swallow me. He came closer and quietly said, "Good-day Ma'am."

I looked up, and seeing a mocking look in his beautiful blue eyes I blushed deeply, reddening my complexion even more. In my confusion and discomfort I blurted out, "At least you smell a little sweeter today."

He grinned, showing his white teeth and the endearing dimple that had so overwhelmed me on his previous visit. I thought him a great deal improved since then – his beard was now neatly trimmed, his hair tidy, and he was dressed in smart new buckskins: in all, quite a devastating handsome man.

"You look and smell pretty good yourself Ma'am", he said, with a hint of laughter in his voice. Flustered, I dropped my gaze and dementedly stirred the washtub stick. As we both fell silent I remembered my manners and mumbled my thanks for the fox fur cape, adding that I really couldn't accept such a valuable gift – but all the while thinking that I'd have to kill anyone who tried to wrest it off me. He assured me that I deserved it. He said that the gift was payment for the loan of my wagon and horses, without which he would not have reached the trading post in time. He went on to say that after trading his furs he'd bought a horse and ridden over to Black Rock to have the best of his fox pelts fashioned into my cape. I wondered as he spoke if he'd found a tart there, but thought it prudent to keep my own thoughts on that.

I was observing him as he talked, thinking how well his Indian blood had mingled with his Scottish ancestry; together they had made a pleasing man. "I've a mind," he said, "to linger in these parts and try my hand at farming, and I understand you might have a room to let here at Station House." I pulled myself together and tried to look as a landlady should, but all the while my heart was singing – he'd said he was planning to stay awhile. "Thank you Lord," I whispered. Deserting the wash tub, I dried my hands and led him indoors to show him a room.

Offering refreshments, I told him to sit in the dining room, smiling at the memory of his previous visit when I'd craftily sat him on the back porch. I brought out two cups with the coffee pot and sat at the table with him. Now that I'd changed into a clean shirt and smoothed back my hair I was feeling calmer, and able to converse with a little more dignity, although my heart was still beating fast enough to be surely heard. Strangely enough we talked like old friends might, and were comfortable with each other. With mischief in his eyes he asked if my man was still out in the fields. "No, he's dead," I said. Now it was his turn to be embarrassed and ill at ease. He apologised for his lack of courtesy, but I smiled and said, "It was a long time ago, and in another world." And for the first time since my return to Canada I told a stranger about William's end, and talked of my three children who lay out on the prairie soil. He saw the rawness of my pain and took my hand in his, and I was comforted.

He told me a little of his own childhood, happily spent in the Cree village until his mother died. When his father came for him he'd tried to hide, not wanting to go with the rough-looking trapper whose words he didn't understand. I felt a sadness for the puzzled little boy that he must have been, and kept his hand in mine. He said he had travelled across most of the Provinces by the time he'd reached maturity, six months being the longest his father had stayed put in any place. He'd had little schooling, but had learnt to read and write one winter, when holed up in a snowbound Alberta shack with a group of other trappers. "I learnt to speak French and Swedish that way too," he grinned.

I had to rise and prepare dinner for my returning lodgers, but it was hard to tear myself away from this man who fascinated me as no other man ever had. He left to collect his belongings from the trading post where he'd stored them, and it was late before he returned. But, as I lay in my bed unable to sleep, I heard him coming down the track, and I felt a sudden surge of happiness that I was under the same roof as him.

He rode away early the next morning to meet a land agent who was to show him available farms in the area. I sorely felt his absence, but with so many chores to catch up on I thought it just as well he was occupied elsewhere. It was dusk when he returned and I was busy feeding passengers from a Montreal-bound train and only had time to nod my head and hand him a plate of stew. He came into the scullery after the train had gone, and found me hard at work with a pile of soiled dishes still to wash. He silently took me by the arm and steered me to sit down on the wooden kitchen stool, and then without a word he rolled up his shirt sleeves and started to wash the remainder of the dishes himself. I tried to protest, but without turning, he said, "Hush your mouth woman, and rest." I was close to tears, which I could have blamed on my being overtired, but I knew it was because of his kindness; it was a long time since anybody had been so concerned for my welfare, and never before had I seen a man at the scullery sink.

He rode out every day in his search for land. Occasionally he would ride out before dawn and not return for three days or more, and just as I was fretting at his absence, fearful that he had gone for good, he would come cantering down the track, his smile as bright as ever, and usually a couple of rabbits or a wild goose hanging from his saddle. I would be a little aloof at first, not wishing to show that I'd missed him, but by suppertime I would have relented, charmed by his easy manner and considerate ways.

He was having difficulty in finding land. It was too expensive for him to buy, and his Cree blood was a handicap when applying for the rental system. I was angry that he was so judged, such a fine man to be denied the chance to work the very soil that his forbears had birthright to. I offered to vouch for him, but he said he wouldn't hide behind a woman's skirt, he would find land on his own merit.

Winter snow was fast approaching and soon he would be forced by the weather to give up his search. Most days now he set his traps, and was keeping the station larder well stocked with meat and fowl. One crisp morning I opened the porch door to find two full blood Indians sat silent on the steps; shocked I ran back inside and fastened the door. When Mac came back midday with a deer across his back they were still sat there, he rushed towards the porch and embraced them both, and they laughed and clasped his hands. Seeing this I too ventured outside to greet them, feeling foolish and very conscious of my own racial ignorance. "My cousins," said Mac, and then they all conversed rapidly in their own tongue.

I offered refreshments, but Mac said there was no time. He had to leave immediately. They had come with bad news, his grandfather was dying and wanted to see him, and it was a long trek to the Cree Village. He quickly gathered his things together, saddled his horse, stopped for a second to wish me well, and then galloped away across the track.

I sat on the steps and cried – would I ever see him again, I wondered – and I realised in that instant that I loved him, how I wished I'd told him so. What if he stayed in the village and never came back, perhaps thinking me indifferent to his gestures of affection? I didn't even know where the Cree village was, and all I could do was pray that he would soon return. After a while I dried my eyes and went back inside; a train was due and I had food to prepare.

Station House, Blue River Halt. 20th of November 1909.

Letting Go

It had been twelve long weeks since Mac had left with his cousins. I had no idea where he'd gone. I knew his grandfather lived up country on an Indian reservation, but had no notion of its location, or had any wish to make enquiries – there was already enough gossip in our locality about us, and I didn't want to fuel it.

I continued with my busy daily routine, caring for my lodgers, and feeding the tired and hungry passengers, although I freely admit I hardly noticed or cared what they ate, my mind being totally preoccupied with thoughts of my handsome half-breed trapper.

When the weeks had stretched well into a new year, I began to accept that he might not be coming back. Inwardly I raged and felt ill used, weeping many tears into my pillow in the privacy of my room. I'd been so certain that his regard for me had equalled mine for him.

Other people must have noticed my depression. Old Sam, in an effort to cheer me suggested I go and pay Mary McDonald a visit, and enjoy a break from the station house. Whilst I was considering it, he, with his usual lack of tact, said he guessed that the half-breed wasn't coming back, and was probably married to some Indian wench by now – all the while watching my face to note any reaction. But I disappointed him, keeping my face inscrutable, and shrugging my shoulders as if what he had said was of no importance. I then handed him a broom and suggested he sweep the platform instead of idly gossiping.

My spirits were low at this time, and in my quieter moments I wondered what I was doing here. Living in an isolated backwater, slaving over a hot stove, and serving endless meals for passing strangers, to whom I was just another railroad worker. My thoughts constantly turned to my two little boys, imagining their daily lives, living in the familiar farmhouse that I too had grown up in. I could imagine them playing the same games that I had once played, running up the main staircase, and then down the narrow back one to confuse my mother as to my whereabouts. I could almost hear their laughter as they chased each other through the tall grass in the fields that I knew so well. At times like this I sorely missed them. In such a low mood I reflected on my sorrows, wondering where the young, carefree girl had gone, she who had first come to this country so full of hope, and a head full of romantic dreams. For the first time I allowed myself to mourn William and his loss.

Mary McDonald, well primed by old Sam, had sent a message asking me to visit for a few days, so leaving Agnes in charge of the station house I set off for my first break since Mac had left. Driving the wagon down the familiar track I felt myself lightening in spirit, and later in the journey a sudden surge of courage led me to halt the horses at the turning that led to our old home.

I couldn't resist the urge that led me down that trail; it was as if my long gone children were calling me to follow it, and so I turned the horses and headed for the homestead, my mind in a turmoil but knowing I had to see my children's resting place again.

My new-found courage almost deserted me when I saw the homestead come into view. A woman came out onto the porch at the sound of visitors, a young baby in her arms. I remembered the times I too had rushed to that same porch, eager for company. As I neared the cabin I realised I had met her before, at one of the barn dances I'd attended. I recollected that she had been new to the area, but I'd had no idea that she and her husband were living on William's place. And I suspected that Mary McDonald, and other friends' sensitivities had kept back that information.

The homestead was looking well cared for, the cabin enlarged, the yard neat and tidy, and the barn re-roofed. I was amazed to see the Christmas pine that William had replanted was now towering above the cabin. The young woman held out her hand in greeting, and said, "I'm Nellie Robson, and you are the lady from the station house." I nodded, my voice too choked to speak, the agitation must have shown in my face as she quickly invited me in, and offered refreshments.

Lost in bitter memories I just stared blankly and then rudely pushed past her, and into the scullery to look out of the window at the rear yard. There was nothing to see other than a neat kitchen garden, and despite her protests I threw open the door and rushed outside, where I stared in dismay at the cleared land. I sank to the ground and beat my hands against my breast. I had no more tears to shed, and my heart ached with the pain that had never gone away.

Without a word the young woman led me back into the cabin and gently sat me down, placed a cup of coffee at my side, and knelt alongside me. Holding my hand in hers she explained that her husband had moved the tiny graves to a more sheltered spot, which she would take me to see when I was feeling a little better. I quickly stood and asked to see them right away, and seeing the determination in my face she took me by the arm and guided me across the yard to a small clearing behind the barn.

Once there I saw a small, well-tended plot surrounded by a white painted picket fence, and there in a carpet of prairie wild flowers were the graves of my three beloved children, each still bearing the wooden crosses that William had so lovingly crafted. Looking more closely I could see a fourth tiny mound that had been overshadowed by a recently planted tree, and turned with enlightenment to Nellie, who was weeping too. I was filled with compassion, and held out my arms to comfort her. This beautiful land could bewitch you, but you always had to beware its cruelty, and the pain it could inflict as you attempted to tame it.

Later I sat and nursed Nellie's baby whilst she prepared a meal for her husband who was due in from the fields. "We moved your children's graves after we'd lost our little one," she explained, "I couldn't have borne staring at them every day from the scullery window, so Daniel, my husband, prepared the little plot you saw." She said she tended it daily, coaxing the flowers to grow, and saying a prayer for my three as well as her own. "I hope you don't mind that we moved them," she anxiously asked. I took her hand and told her how grateful I was for her loving care, and how I would always pray for her lost child along with my own.

I hugged her new-born baby, loving that special baby smell that teased my memory, and brought back the long-buried recollections of nursing my own. Whilst here at the homestead I was keenly feeling their loss, and also the enforced absence of my two boys, who were so far away across the ocean.

Her husband came in from the fields, a robust young man whom I immediately liked and trusted. After our introduction I thanked him for the care of my children's graves. He blushed a fiery red, and mumbled that he hoped that anyone would have done the same, and how he thought it a comfort to his wife to have my three lie with their own little one. Nellie and I shed a few more tears at his words, and then I said I'd best be on my way to the McDonalds' place before darkness fell. I hugged Nellie tightly, and kissed the baby goodbye. We both knew that we had forged a bond that neither time nor distance could ever break. Daniel rode behind me as far as the main track, where we parted. He told me to visit anytime, but as I urged the horses forward I knew I would never go to the homestead again.

Blue River. 1st of March 1910.

A Special Visitation

The few days I had spent with Mary McDonald and my unscheduled visit to William's homestead had helped to lift my gloom. My mind was at ease at last about my three babes' final resting place. I had thought it long dispersed by the prairie winds or perhaps disturbed by wild dogs. But now, having seen the well-cared for little plot, I felt I could rest easy, knowing that the young couple would tend to them along with their own.

Mary's cheerful company and her brood of lively children had soon raised my spirits, and whilst making a whole year's supply of pickles we gossiped happily together, and I was able to unburden my feelings about Mac's apparent desertion. Not one to mince her words, Mary told me it was all for the best, advising that a half-cast trapper was not what she would call a suitable match. "But I love him and can't understand why he's not come back, I was so sure that he had feelings for me." "Oh yes," Mary said, "I saw with my own eyes the way he looked at you. Any fool, never mind the whole of Blue River, could see the way he felt about you."

Somewhat cheered and armed with half a dozen jars of pickle, and Mary's special tomato chutney, I made the return journey home with a lighter heart. I also had the company and lively chatter of fourteen-year-old Terence McDonald, who was heading to the Halt to be apprenticed to the blacksmith there. I had been specially charged by Mary to keep an eye on him. And this time I'd managed to drive past the familiar turn off with no pangs of regret, knowing now that it was in good hands.

It seemed that all had gone well at the Station House in my absence: between them Agnes and Old Sam had fed and watered two train-loads of passengers without mishap. Agnes had much improved in her work since her idle, sour-faced husband had walked out on her last fall. In truth I think she was much happier without him; he had seemed a bullying type of man and she deserved better.

Old Sam was quick to tell me that he'd had to chase off two pesky Indian varmints who had been hanging around the platform for a day or two. "They went pretty fast when I threatened put my boot up their backsides," he said, in his usual coarse way. I ignored him, but my heart started to beat a little faster wondering if they had come with a message from Mac. Now I was annoyed that I'd not been there. Perhaps he had needed my help and had sent his cousins to fetch me.

My mind was racing and I felt angry with Old Sam for sending them away. I coldly told him that in future I would like any further Indian visitors to be offered some refreshments, and for him to have the courtesy to inform me of their presence. But sadly we saw no further sign of them, although I daily looked for their return.

Life settled back into the old routine: trains coming and going, meals to cook and serve, washing to do, and all the endless jobs that made up my daily life. My birthday came and went un-noticed other than the much treasured letters that came a week early from my darling boys. The night of my birthday I stood in front of my bedroom mirror and really looked at myself for the first time in many years. My figure was still trim and my hair had kept its darkness, but I looked unsatisfied and unfulfilled. Here I was, little more than a cook, slaving away for the Canadian Pacific Railroad in a remote Station House. I could see no future, and more painful than anything was the loneliness I felt. I'd had plenty of male attention since coming back to Canada, sometimes more than I had liked. I had not been flattered by all the proposals I'd received; women were scarce in the Province, and a woman of any age or appearance could easily find a husband. If I was honest with myself I knew that my heart had been lost the day that Mac had walked down the track and flashed his irresistible smile at me. I turned away from the mirror and berated myself for being such a fool.

The 'Empress of Canada' was due in the very next day. She was a new train on her maiden voyage from Montreal to Vancouver. I had been warned that the directors of the railroad would be aboard, and I was determined to present Blue River Halt to its best advantage. I made a special effort with the menu, and had Agnes put clean white tablecloths on the dining tables instead of the normal scrubbed pine. Old Sam swept the platform spotless and polished the lamps till they shone. I personally inspected the rest rooms making sure that fresh soap and clean towels were laid out ready for our prestigious visitors. As a final touch I placed folded napkins on each table – I wanted my employers to see that I was used to finer living.

We were all waiting on the platform when she arrived – in fact the whole of Blue River Halt had turned out to greet her. As she came down the track the driver blew her piercing whistle and all the passengers were leaning out of the window waving to us. The engine was really beautiful, its proud brass funnels gleaming in the late afternoon sunshine. The traditional, solid cow catcher at the front looked unnecessary for such an impressive powerful machine; I couldn't imagine any animal challenging its splendour. The company director and his wife were on board, and as the conductor helped them onto the platform I felt suddenly shabby, even though I was dressed in my best Sunday wear. She looked so smart and fashionable it made me realise just how dowdy I had become. However, they were very pleasant and congratulated me on the station's tidy appearance as I escorted them to the rest rooms.

Passengers were looking for the dining room so Agnes and I quickly made for the kitchen to dish up dinner. We were too busy to note any of the other passengers and it was as I turned to serve the director and his wife that I saw him standing at the door. For one brief moment our eyes met and he smiled his special mischievous smile at me, but I could see even at that distance that his eyes were serious, and full of love.

And then I did something I had never in my life done before, and in full view of the director and his wife too – I simply fainted clean away.

Station House. 3rd of April 1910.

A Proposal

I came round from my faint to find myself lying on the sofa in the parlour with Agnes frantically waving smelling salts under my nose, and an anxious-looking Mac kneeling at my side, rubbing my cold hands in his. My blouse had been unbuttoned at the neck, and my corsets loosened – both by Agnes, I sincerely hoped.

Seeing my recovery Agnes said she would return to see to the passengers' needs as the train would soon be departing. She could have been talking a foreign language for all the notice I took. I had taken leave of my senses and had no notion of what she was talking about; my attention was totally taken by the man at my side. He bent down and gently kissed my cheek, which threw me in even more confusion, and I still can't believe what I did next when I brazenly pulled his head to mine and kissed him full on the lips. To hide my embarrassment I started to scold him for his long absence, but he put his finger to my mouth, gave me his devastating smile, and then quite simply asked me to marry him. In truth I nearly fainted again, but instead sat bolt upright and glared at him. "How dare you," I gasped. "You disappear for months on end, and then stroll back in and presume I've been waiting for your return." His smile broadened, and keeping tight hold of my hands he started to laugh. "I can see you haven't changed," he said, and then promptly kissed me again.

Accepting that by now my reputation had been torn to shreds I told him I would accept his offer, otherwise I would never again be able to hold up my head in Blue River Halt, and then I spoilt my dignified reply by kissing him back. We sat an age cuddling and whispering endearments, but a sudden blast from the departing train brought us back to the real world, and I became mindful of my duties. We rushed out onto the platform just in time to see the back of the Empress of Canada as she majestically left the station. The director lifted his top hat to me as he waved from the rear viewing platform, and delirious with happiness I blew him a kiss.

Mac helped Agnes and I to clear the dining room and kitchen, and then once she had left for home we went out onto the platform, where we sat close together and talked. Mac told me what he had been doing all those long months that he'd been away. On arriving at the reservation with his cousins he had found his grandfather very sick, but had sat by his side throughout the next day, and well into the night, during which the old man breathed his last and peacefully passed away.

Mac had stayed on at the reservation for a further month, joining in with the traditional tribal funeral that had sped his grandfather to find his everlasting hunting ground. I was enthralled by Mac's description of the tribal mourning rituals, totally unlike anything I'd ever experienced. And I began to understand some of the background that had helped to shape this complex man whom I so dearly loved.

Afterwards, when clearing his grandfather's cabin, he'd found official land deeds that proved his ownership of a tract of land many miles away from the reservation, a thousand acres of prairie land in the province of Alberta. It had been purchased many years earlier by Jimmie McKenzie and put in the safe keeping of Mac's grandfather, who had on his approaching death wanted Mac to be aware of his inheritance. He had thought him too unsettled in his youth to take advantage of his father's legacy, but felt it was now time that Mac should lay claim to the land.

After the mourning period was over, he had decided to travel to Alberta and prove his right to the property. Leaving the Indian camp early in the new year he had ridden cross country, travelling as many days as the weather had allowed, and holing up in isolated cabins when the snow proved too fierce. He had instructed his cousins to ride to the Halt to tell me of his mission, and to explain that he would be back with me as soon as he possibly could. He was dismayed that I'd not received his message, and had suffered such doubts about his intentions. He cuddled me awhile to show exactly what his intentions were.

Excitedly gripping my hand, he told me that the land was everything he'd ever wanted: good prairie soil, virgin as yet, but crying out to be cultivated. He'd had to spend a further six weeks in Edmonton endeavouring to stake his claim to his father's land. Officials had been dubious about his right of ownership, and had hindered his quest. But in the end the deeds and his birthright had proved him the new owner.

"And that's what kept me away from you for so long," he said. "I sent for my cousins to join me, and we cleared some of the land, and now I have left them working on a cabin that I'm hoping you will soon be sharing with me."

I was very happy for him. I knew how important it was to him to have some land in this country that he so cherished, and also his burning desire to place some roots in the soil of his ancestors. I hugged him tight and promised I would go wherever he wanted me to. My own heart had soared, to live back on my beloved prairies, and to be with the man that I so dearly loved would be more than I'd ever hoped for. And now I knew why I had always recognised that my true destiny had been here in Canada: it was because Mac had been here all this time, waiting for me.

Station House, Blue River Halt. 3rd of April 1910.

A Station Wedding

I married Mac on a beautiful sunny day in early May. We had the ceremony on the platform at the station house. A preacher came up the line on an outward train especially to marry us. It was the first ever wedding in Blue River Halt, and people came from miles away to see us wed. In fact the whole population of Blue River seemed to be crowded on that platform.

I wore a simple navy dress with white trimmings that I had made myself, copying a magazine picture that a railway guest from Montreal had left in the dining room. I could see by the appreciative look that Mac gave me as I walked onto the platform that it met with his approval, and despite the warmth of the day I had slipped the silver fox fur that he had once given me around my shoulders.

We both wore the wide wrist bands which had Cree tribal images engraved on their smooth panned gold, gifts from Mac's mother's people, and brought down to the station house the night before by his cousins. They couldn't be persuaded to stay for our wedding, but promised to visit us later when we were settled on the farm. I was used to their coming and going now, and they felt more at ease with me too, even giving me, much to my amusement, an Indian name. I was now known to the tribe as White Flying Bird, and Mac would use this name when we were alone.

As I walked the length of the platform on Old Sam's arm to stand beside Mac in front of the preacher, my mind was full of rapid scrambled thoughts and flashing visions of the past: the boys back on the farm in Derbyshire, where they were happy and content, and my other three, never far from my thoughts, but now with a grudging acceptance of their loss, and fleetingly a brief memory of my other wedding day, when young and full of hope I gave myself to William.

But as I stood alongside Mac, and took his arm and looked into his clear blue eyes that were so full of love for me, I knew that these past memories were just a pathway that had led me to his side. I gave my vows to him with all my heart, promising to be there for him in sickness and health, and he gave me his with such sincerity and trust that tears fell unchecked down my face. As he placed the gold band on my finger he kissed them away.

We had such a party, so many people there, that it spilled out into the street. Mary McDonald and Agnes had done us proud, with tables laden with food which had been added to by the home-baked pies and roasted fowl that the guests had brought. The two-tiered iced cake that I myself had laboured on took pride of place in the centre of the long trestle table.

The celebrations went on throughout the night, long after Mac and I had left on the late evening Vancouver-bound train. It had been a wrench handing my bunch of station keys over to Agnes. I had always relished my position as station proprietor, and had some regret for its ending. I had recommended Agnes for the post, she was more than adequate, and had become a new woman since her idle, domineering husband had left her. She hugged me close with tears in her eyes, but I'm sure she was itching to get on with her new responsibilities, and to see us go.

The Pacific railroad company had been more than generous, giving me a month's salary as a leaving bonus, and also two free return tickets for our honeymoon in Vancouver. Mac and I stood arm in arm on the rear viewing platform as we waved goodbye to the population of Blue River Halt, and the many wonderful people who had stood by me in my darkest days.

I felt strange when the conductor called me Mrs McKenzie as he showed us to our sleeping berths. Earlier I had been amused when the preacher had called Mac by his full name – James Alistair McKenzie – it just didn't seem like Mac, although he had smirked at mine too – Edith Gertrude Goodwin Jerram.

I was excited by the journey, never having been to Vancouver or crossed the Rockies. But I was even more excited when we arrived in the beautiful city. The rail line ran through the city's main thoroughfare straight down to the waterfront, and I was amazed by the busy paved streets thronged with fashionably-dressed crowds. The well-stocked shops were a never ending pleasure; if it had not been for boring Mac I could have spent my days there. These few days together were wonderful: we explored the city, dined in pleasant eating houses, visited the theatre, and spent the nights wrapped in each other's arms in the small guest house that Agnes's sister had recommended. We were overwhelmed by the intensity of our feelings for each other, and I was tremendously happy.

We both enjoyed our stay in Vancouver but were eager to get back to the prairies. I longed to see our farm and to make a home of the cabin that had been newly built. We stayed over in Blue River Halt to collect our belongings, and after loading the wagon and saying our goodbyes yet again, we headed the horses east, taking the trail that would lead us towards Alberta. It was a long and tiring journey. Sometimes we slept in the wagon, lying close together under the stars, and despite the distant howling of wolves I felt safe wrapped in Mac's arms. Occasionally we stayed overnight at lonely homesteads where the women of the household would be overjoyed to have female company. I understood their pleasure, remembering my own lonely days out on the prairie when William had worked away.

At last we reached Edmonton and, stabling the wagon and horses, took time to rest, and take advantage of hot baths and a comfortable bed. We also stocked up on provisions and farm implements before leaving, as it would be quite a while before we returned to a township.

It took us another two days to reach our new home, and as we approached the boundaries of our land I could see the hard work that Mac had done whilst he had been so long away: already there were fences in place, and a track marked out to point the way to the new cabin. I felt guilty for having doubted him during those long months he had been gone.

We turned a corner on the grassy track, and there on a slight rise in the ground was the cabin that he had built. It stood proud and welcoming, its new timbers clean and straight. It was much bigger than I'd imagined, and I turned and hugged Mac to show my delight. Beaming at my approval he drove the wagon up to the door, jumped off, and then with no further ado lifted me down and climbed the porch steps with me still in his arms. Pushing open the door he carried me in, and once inside placed me gently on my feet, and holding me tightly he whispered, "Welcome, White Flying Bird."

I looked up at my handsome new husband with pride and love, and I knew I had come home at last.

The McKenzie Place. 20th of May 1910.

A Barn Topping Party

Our new barn was almost completed. Mac had laboured hard all summer, cutting the timber and preparing the framework. I too had done my part by smoothing down the wood, and the fetching and carrying as required.

But now we needed help with the roofing of it, essential before winter set in. Our nearest neighbour, a German man called Erich Seebach, called in on his way to the store, and suggested we hold a barn topping party. Seemingly this was the custom in these parts, with all the neighbours gathering together, and whilst the menfolk roofed the barn, the women and children prepared a feast to celebrate its completion.

Mac was doubtful, as he was a proud man who didn't accept favours easily, but Erich said we would soon be asked to return the goodwill, with invitations from others to participate in their roofing ceremonies.

I was eager to make acquaintance with other women; I missed the easy feminine relationships I'd had in Blue River Halt. I think for this reason alone Mac was persuaded to have a topping party. Erich agreed to pass the news around that coming Sunday whilst at church, and would let the storekeeper know too, so that the invitation could be more widely spread.

We arranged it for a week Saturday which would allow people time to hear the news. I was excited – it would be the first party we had given together, and I wanted it to be perfect. I was already making lists of food to be prepared, but Mac cautioned me not to build my hopes too high. He pointed out that we had been here nearly four months now, and invitations from the neighbourhood had been few and far between. Other than Erich who was a widower, and our other neighbours the Williamson family, we'd had no other visitors or been especially welcomed into the area. Even when meeting people at the store I'd noticed a distinct lack of cordiality. I was not so naive as not to realise the reason why. I was aware that some people were prejudiced, and not eager to entertain a half-breed Cree in their home, and that possibly they looked on me as a fallen woman to have actually married one.

Still I liked to think that most people were of good principle, and wouldn't hesitate to help a neighbour, whatever his race or creed. So in good cheer I baked bread and scones, made meat pies, and prepared enough food for a virtual horde. Come Saturday morning I rose at sunlight to stoke the stove, and make ready for our guests. Mac did his own chores, and then finalised preparations for the barn roofing.

By midday the food was spoiling, and the roofing timbers still lay on the ground where he had earlier laid them. I sat on the porch fretting that no one was coming, and felt the anger rising in me at our neighbour's disdain. Early afternoon and only Erich had come. To be fair, young Owen Williamson had called earlier to offer his parent's apologies. His father was laid up with a chronic backache and not fit to work, but Grace had sent a basket of freshly baked rolls and a boiling of sweet corn.

So much food and no one to eat it, and the barn still without its roof. Erich volunteered to help, but Mac declined his well-meant offer, saying the beams were too heavy for just the two of them to lift. So, after a sharing a hearty meal, he left for home.

My heart sank once we were alone. I could see that Mac was inwardly hurting at the slight our neighbours had given. I think he was more upset by my distress than at any racial intent to him. But I was seething with rage at their petty ways, and had little sleep that night.

My fury had not cooled by morning, and I asked Mac to harness the horses as I intended to drive to Red Deer and attend the church service there, which I had on occasions done before. Thinking the outing would calm my mood, Mac did as I asked, lifting me up onto the wagon. He hugged me, and bade me not to be upset on his behalf. I kissed him soundly, and then took up the reins and sped off up the track.

The little church was full and the service in full flow when I arrived. Not deterred, I picked up my Sunday skirts and marched up the aisle. I begged the padre's pardon but asked if I could say a few words to his congregation – I looked long and hard at them, these prairie people who prided themselves on their hospitality and generosity. And then, with the utmost contempt in my voice, I said exactly what I had come to say. "Call yourselves Christians, not one of you is fit to lick my husband's boots. He's a decent honest man whose mother was a Cree, and they too are honourable good people." I then thanked the padre for his patience and walked head held high to the door, but turned once again to face his open-mouthed flock, and added that they should be ashamed of themselves, and then suggested that seeing as they were in church they should get on their knees, and ask God to forgive them for being such mean-minded, petty people.

Once outside I clambered back onto the wagon, shaking a little now at my own daring, but feeling better for having said my piece. I pulled on the reins and headed for home.

By two o'clock the yard was full of wagons, and still more coming down the track. The menfolk were swarming up the ladders heaving the heavy timbers aloft, and the sound of chattering voices and the banging of nails was resounding across the yard. The women were busy laying out the dishes of food they had brought, and even the padre was there, his shirt sleeves rolled up as he offered his advice as to the exact slant of the roof. Children in a party mood were running around the paddock like young colts set free. The babies were laid to sleep in the shade, and the old people joined them and talked of the past, and shared their memories.

Mac had looked quite bewildered at this sudden influx of neighbours, but was soon up in the air astride a rafter, gladly welcoming the unexpected workforce. I was overjoyed to see the ready acceptance that the men were giving him, and knew that once they were all acquainted his own ready charm and easy manner would win their friendship.

The barn roof was on before nightfall, but the party went on well into the early hours. The hungry men had devoured the food, and quenched their thirst with the barrel of ale that had appeared from the back of one of the wagons. And soon an old granddad took up his fiddle and the barn floor was cleared for dancing. I noted that no female, be them young or old, refused my handsome husband's request to take his arm and dance with him. In fact I felt a little jealous to see them so rapt in attention to his every word. But I too was enjoying the female company, and was revelling in the warmth of their harmless gossip, and the exchange of family recipes. During the evening we received countless invitations to visit and to take supper at various homesteads, and also to attend a wedding in the late fall. Thankfully nobody mentioned my visit to the church.

As the last wagon left dawn was breaking, and Mac and I stood arm in arm in the barn, admiring its smart new roof. He pulled me close and looked intently in my eyes and asked, "What mischief were you up to this morning Mrs McKenzie?"

Blushing a little, I replied, "None at all. I guess it was just one of God's miracles."

The McKenzie Place. 30th of September 1910.

Expectations

Mac was overjoyed when we found I was with child. He whooped and danced around the yard with excitement at the news. I laughed, and said he looked as if he was doing a Cree war dance, but he said it was more of a crazy man's celebration.

I knew he loved children; he was always a popular figure with our neighbours' numerous offspring, never too busy to stop and carve a whistle for the boys, or a miniature doll for the admiring little girls, who would flock to his side at every gathering we attended. At parties I would look with envy at his ease of manner with the youths who so obviously copied his every move. I always felt such regret that my own two boys had no part of this caring man's life.

This would be my sixth child, and yet as now my arms were empty. And despite my shared happiness with Mac I was secretly afraid for this coming baby. There was still a grieving part of me that forever silently mourned the three I'd buried. And although for the present my boys were lost to me I knew they were well and safe in England. But this new babe would be born here on the prairies, which I painfully knew could hide a harsh and cruel side behind their enchanting horizons.

For Mac, never was a baby more eagerly awaited. He spent many hours making a cradle fit for a prince, carving beautiful tribal symbols into the lavishly-polished pine. He spent the long winter months making toys and dozens of play bricks, each one carefully smoothed and lettered. I sewed nightgowns and knitted warm jackets, which Mac would hold up and marvel at their size.

I so hoped that this babe would be a boy because Mac would make him a wonderful father: he would teach him how to hunt, and all the trapping skills his own father had shown him. But Mac said he would be happy to have a daughter, and would feel very proud to have two McKenzie women on his arm when visiting.

For the first few months I had been in good health, positively blooming, so I was told by the doctor that Mac had insisted I should see. But as we went into early spring my body grew heavy and my spirits fell. I felt a strange sense of disquiet and foreboding, and as my time grew near I had a sudden premonition of disaster. I tried for Mac's sake to cast these feelings off, as I could see he was worried by my depression. He would rush back to the cabin in the middle of his spring planting just to check on me. I'd always had strange apprehensive feelings, often foreseeing some event or misfortune long before it occurred. My father used to say that I took after his grandmother, who had been known locally as the old witch because of her visionary and psychic experiences. But I preferred to think that it was my condition that was making me so fearful. Mac did everything in his power to calm me. He insisted I rest whilst he cooked and cleaned, and even washed the sheets to save me from undue exertion.

I had never been so cherished and thanked God every day for my good fortune. I only wished that this pregnancy didn't make me feel so sad. Grace Williamson came over to sit with me whenever she could spare the time; she was a great comfort, and would take hold of my hands and tell me how much better I was going to feel once I held this baby in my arms. She too had lost a child and had some understanding of my fears. But I couldn't explain, even to her, this perception I had of inevitable tragedy.

My due date came and passed with Mac quite beside himself with anxiety – strangely enough I was now calm and composed, ready to accept whatever destiny had in store for me. I would sit out on the porch watching Mac working in the yard, or if he was out on the land I would put on my sun bonnet and walk out to where he was, and he in panic would down his tools, thinking me in labour.

The baby was still very active and its violent kicking would make Mac grin with delight when he placed his hands on my swollen squirming stomach. We had been joined by Hetty Watson, a widowed farmer's wife, who had delivered most of the neighbourhood children, and had agreed to come and stay for my confinement.

She had moved in the day before my due date and had made herself at home, so much so that Mac had found himself banished to the barn to sleep. There was no way Hetty would have allowed him to see her in her nightwear.

A week had passed since my due date, and the relationship between husband and midwife was getting very strained. He had been reduced to climbing through the bedroom window to kiss me goodnight, and I feared that if this baby didn't hurry Hetty would pack her bag and leave, such was the discord.

And then, as babies do, it took us all by surprise. It was as I stood at the barn door watching Mac milk the cow that my waters broke and a sudden stab of pain overcame me. An ever-watchful Mac sent the milk bucket flying as he ran to offer his support. Back in the cabin Hetty took charge, ordering Mac to put the kettle to boil and me to bed. And then my labour started, with such a vengeance that at times I wished to die. Hetty, skilled as she was, seemed at a loss to deal with the hours of agony that I was enduring, and still the baby wouldn't come. At some stage Mac could stand my suffering no longer, and saddled his horse and rode to fetch the doctor.

My memory is hazy about the time it took, but I remember the doctor arriving and the concerned look on his face as he examined me. Somehow together we forced that baby out, and at last blessedly the pain stopped, and I sunk back onto Mac's arms as he lay me on my pillow. Despite Hetty's disproval he had been at my side since returning with the doctor. My life's blood had started to seep away, and it was only the doctor's skill that saved my life. But I needed to see my baby, and had not yet heard it cry – so Mac came to my side, cradling the most perfect little girl. She was beautifully formed, with a mass of dark curly hair, but she was also sleeping, a sleep from which she was never going to awake.

The McKenzie place. 31st of May 1911.

The Fugitive

We had heard the dogs barking in the night, but Mac had thought it probably a lone fox searching for food. Next morning he looked for its tracks but found no trace, although the barn door was slightly ajar, and he knew it had been closed the night before. Suspicions of an intruder, he came back into the cabin to get his gun and warned me to stay indoors.

Anxious for his safety I stood on the veranda and watched him stealthily creep up to the barn, where he threw open the door and rushed inside, his gun cocked and ready to fire. I heard no shot or sound of raised voices, and, concerned for Mac's safety, took up the heavy poker and decided to investigate for myself. As I reached the barn door Mac was just coming out, and smiled at the sight of me with a weapon in my hand. Putting his finger to his lips he took my arm and led the way into the dim barn, and there curled up on a bed of hay was a young boy fast asleep.

Sensing our presence he woke, and quickly got to his feet, and made as if to flee, but Mac held him tight, and then seeing the look of terror on his face gently sat him down on a bale of straw. On closer inspection he looked no more than a child, and an ill-used one at that. He seemed half starved and poorly clad, his feet were covered in weeping sores, and the boots he'd cast off onto the barn floor were fit only for the fire. He was plainly petrified, and obviously expecting to be punished. My heart went out to him, and I knelt by his side to tell him he wouldn't be harmed, that we would help him if he told us where he was heading, and how he had got here in this wretched state.

But first I said, he must eat something and rest, and then he could tell us what I fully expected to be a sorry tale. Mac helped him back to the cabin; the poor lad could barely walk. Once inside he drank his fill of milk, and demolished a loaf of bread spread with wild strawberry jam. He was of smallish build with a pockmarked skin, not the most handsome of lads, but surely deserving of a more kindly treatment than he had clearly received.

He brightened up a little after his meal, and recognising that Mac and I meant him no harm got almost cheerful in his manner. He was not so happy when I suggested that he would be better for a good wash and a soak of his poor feet, but realising I was determined he submitted to having his face and hands thoroughly scrubbed. He looked distinctly more presentable after my ministrations, and once he was newly dressed in an old shirt of Mac's, that on his small frame almost reached to the floor, I felt he might be more inclined to tell us his tale. And indeed, as I'd suspected, it was a sad one.

Ben was his name, and he was not sure of his age, but thought he was about thirteen years old. He was originally from the Old Country, and I guessed by the lilt in his voice that it was probably Wales. He had a vague memory of his mother and an elder sister, and he knew that he wasn't an orphan, but had been shipped to Canada with a group of foundling children when still in short pants. He believed it was a church group that had sent him as he had a recollection of nuns taking him aboard ship. After reaching these shores he and the others were taken by train to Calgary, where they were chosen by people who had offered to give them a home. At this point he seemed to hesitate and was close to tears, but with Mac's encouragement he continued, saying it had been an elderly farming couple who had chosen him, and without any further investigation by his carers he was put on to a wagon and whisked away across the prairies to an unknown destination.

The poor boy had no idea where he was, and had no more contact with the church society that had delivered him there. He said the farmer had been hard on him, and the wife would beat him with a copper stick if she thought him slacking. He had to work from dawn to dusk, and was made to sleep in the outhouse with the dogs. He had endured this dreadful treatment for a number of years, but after a final vicious beating he had become determined to escape and for weeks hid saved scraps of food to take with him. He seized his chance when the travelling man called at the farm to take an order, and hid in the back of the wagon under some bales of cloth, not caring where he went, so long as it was many miles away from the farm where he had been so ill-treated. After twenty miles or more he was discovered by the travelling man, who insisted he get out of the wagon, and who then drove off, leaving him on the track alone. Walking aimlessly for several days, he had eventually seen our chimney smoke, and headed in that direction, arriving late that night, and had bedded down in the barn intending to be away by dawn.

I was in tears myself when he'd finished telling his sad story, and Mac too was hiding some emotion. We told him he could stay awhile with us and gain some strength, and meanwhile we would make some enquiries about getting help for him. He seemed content with this decision and hobbled off happily after Mac to watch him milk the cow.

Left to my own thoughts, I was incensed by the injustice of such cruelty on behalf of the farmer, and the people who had shipped him here. I had read of young children coming to Canada to either be adopted, or as workers on the prairie farms, and knew of one such lad who lived with a neighbour a few miles distant, but he was made much of by the family and considered as a son. There had been a lot of criticism in the British papers, which my sister sent cuttings of, thinking them of interest to me. The church and private adoption societies were being censured by people who were unhappy with their methods of transporting children to Canada. In the beginning I think it was approved by the government, hoping to give destitute youngsters a new start in life. But it was made known that some of the children were not orphans, and had only found themselves in charity homes, or even the workhouse because of family misfortune. These same children were being spirited away without their parents' consent, and furthermore there was disproval of the way they were distributed once reaching Canada, with no checks on the people who were taking them in, and no follow up of their treatment, in what to most of them would be an alien society.

I had not fully believed what I'd read in the cuttings, knowing newspapers tended to exaggerate social issues. But now having met one of these unfortunate children, and seen for myself the damage that had been inflicted on him, I was aghast at their treatment and vowed to write my own letter to the Canadian press.

Ben stayed with us for a month, and we found him a good lad, polite and helpful, and each day he blossomed, and with loving care soon lost that cowed, fearful look. Mac had made discreet enquiries when next he went to the store, but no one had reported a missing boy and we thought that maybe he had travelled further than he'd realised, or the farmer and his wife were not anxious to be known.

He was a bright boy, who with some education could find a worthwhile job. I encouraged him to learn to write his name, and to work at his letters so that one day he could write to his mother to tell her where he was. Privately, I thought she must have abandoned him a long time ago. He had told us that he would like to learn a trade, but would prefer to be in or near a township as he was not over fond of the isolation of living on the prairies.

Mac travelled up to Wainwright and spoke to a lawyer he knew who practised in the town. He told him of Ben's history, and the ill treatment he had suffered since coming to Canada. And quite rightly the lawyer was shocked, said he had heard of similar cases, and it was not the right way to populate the province. He promised to talk to some reputable citizens and to try and find a good home and trade for

Ben, asking Mac to bring the lad with him the following week when he hoped to have good news for them.

I insisted on journeying with them as I wanted to make sure he would be in good hands. The lad's eyes lit up when we reached the town, not the largest one in the province, but it had shops and a busy thoroughfare, which was a treat for me too. The Williamson's eldest boy was taking care of our homestead, so we were going to book into a lodging house and stay a couple of nights to see Ben settled.

The lawyer, true to his word, had spread the news of Ben's plight, and had received two offers of a home for the lad. One was an elderly couple whose own family had fled the nest, and who liked the idea of having a young one to care for again. The other home offered included a chance to learn a trade too, as it was with the local farrier. Ben was fond of animals, and it would be a good opportunity for him. We went along with him to visit them both, and although the old people were a kindly couple I think he preferred the other offer, as the blacksmith and his wife were younger with two sons near to Ben's age.

The following day he went off happily to start his new life with them, and having had conversation with the couple I felt he would have a good Christian home, and be treated well. If only all of those poor children shipped over here would be lucky enough to find such a good family to take them in. I believe the majority did, and were growing up to be content, and have useful lives. It was just a few, whose supposed benefactors abused and neglected them.

Having seen Ben so comfortably settled, and having had my fill of town, Mac and I headed back home to the peace and quiet of the farm.

The McKenzie Place, 27th of August 1911.

The Indian Camp

I was very excited when Mac offered to take me to Banff for the Indian Festivities. He had told me so much about the activities that went on there, that I was eager to see them for myself.

The Festivities were an established meeting place for the Cree and Stoney Indians who would set up camp for the festival's duration. This enabled them to meet up with relatives, renew friendships, and on occasions ignite old feuds.

Mac had happy memories of going there as a child with his Cree mother. The family would travel from their Reservation down to Banff, and on reaching the camp would set up a traditional tepee alongside others of their tribe. The camp would be bustling with activity, the women cooking on open fires, whilst their menfolk sat in the shade smoking, and swapping tales of previous camps. The younger men would swagger around the town dressed in their festival finery of fringed buckskin leggings and soft-soled, beaded moccasins, preening themselves and showing off to the bashful girls, who, whilst helping their mothers cook would cast sideways flirtatious glances at the flaunting young braves.

As a youngster Mac had run wild with the other children, supposedly gathering wood for the fires, but usually exploring the camp and renewing acquaintance with cousins not seen since the previous year.

There was always great anticipation at the start of the festivities, with everyone joining the parade dressed in their tribal best. This would be followed by days of horse racing, foot races, and wrestling. The races would be greatly anticipated and strongly fought, with much rivalry amongst the tribes.

After the Williamson's eldest boy had arrived to keep an eye on the farm, Mac and I set off for Banff. The journey was an adventure in itself. Since coming to the farm we had hardly left it, other than to visit neighbours or make our monthly trip to Red Deer for provisions. But now we were travelling cross-country through some of the most beautiful scenery I had ever seen – miles of magnificent landscape that made you feel quite insignificant, and in awe of such powerful creation. Come nightfall we tethered the horses and slept in the wagon, and continued on our way at first light. At times I felt we were the only two human beings left in the world, and I treasured that feeling.

On arrival in Banff that solitude quickly dispersed: the town was teeming with people. It seemed as if the whole of Canada's Indian population had converged upon it. I was amazed at how many people seemed to know Mac. They ran alongside the wagon, calling out to him. We stabled the horses, and left on foot for the camping grounds on the edge of town. I was amazed at first sight of them – seemingly acres of land dotted with tepees as far as the eye could see, some artistically painted, others simply old canvas sheets wrapped around stakes. Indians were milling everywhere, and the elderly sat in groups by their fireside, inscrutable as they smoked pipes and watched the world go by.

Mac was hailed by a group of youngsters who rushed to take his hand to lead him to the family camp, but they held back when they saw me and seemed at a loss to know how to proceed. They were quickly sent on their way by a giant of a man dressed in traditional Indian clothing, who stepped forward to clasp Mac in his arms. This was Chief Bear's-Paw, Mac's maternal uncle. After briefly conversing in Cree language he turned to me, and I found myself lifted off the floor and held in a tight embrace, with Mac laughing at the shocked expression on my face.

I was then introduced to the rest of the numerous family, and countless faces and names were lost to me as I tried to acknowledge each and every one, only registering the two cousins whom I recognized from their visits to the station house. I was feeling overwhelmed by so much attention, and the babble of voices that I found difficult to understand.

Mac instinctively sensed my discomfort and kept me close until I felt more calm. We were then shown a tepee which had been newly built for us with a sparkling white canvas that was decorated with paintings of deer and buffalo. Mac took me to one side and asked if I was happy with this arrangement; he said he would take a room for us at a lodging house if I felt it more comfortable. Just for a second or two I visualised the hot bath and relaxing bed that a rented room could offer, but I could see that was not an alternative, how hurt Mac's relatives would be if I turned my back on their hospitality. I also reminded myself that I had come to the camp to discover as much as I could about Cree customs, and to get to know Mac's family. So I graciously thanked Bear's-Paw and stepped inside the tepee that was to be my home for the next three days. I was pleasantly surprised by its spacious interior and the brightness of the white canvas which allowed the sun to illuminate the whole area. The floor was covered by animal skins and more were piled high to form a soft bed. In all very cosy and I was sure Mac and I would be quite snug. I realised later that we were favoured in having a tepee to ourselves as most were home to whole families.

We had arrived just in time for the grand parade which was the start of the festivities. Mac found us a good viewpoint in Banff's main street, and I was enthralled by the whole colourful scenario. Many white people had journeyed to marvel at it too, and were taking photographs of the brightly-dressed Indians, and throwing sweets to the children who scrabbled on the dusty floor to find them. I waved and cheered as I saw Mac's uncle on a white horse leading the Crees. He wore a full-feathered head-dress with war paint on his face, and an exquisite beaded waistcoat above his buckskin leggings. He saw us in the crowd and waved his tomahawk in recognition. I thought he looked fearsome and wouldn't have liked to have been his enemy. I asked Mac that had he been a full breed and we had met in a previous life, if would he have scalped me; he grinned and whispered in my ear the forfeit he would have had me pay instead. I blushed and hoped that no one had overheard him.

I loved sleeping in the tepee. It was soothing to lie on our bed of furs and watch the stars that we could see twinkling through the top of the criss-crossed poles that formed its framework. The next day I had offered to help the women prepare the food we ate, but they giggled and pushed me away. At times I felt most uncomfortable, as Mac was often with his cousins preparing the horses for the afternoon races, and I was left to wander alone around the camp, and Cree and Stoney alike would stare at me, wondering what a white woman was doing in an Indian camp. But when the races were on and I embraced Mac's cousin in the excitement of his winning, I received many disparaging looks from the white folk who had come to watch.

I felt more at ease in the evenings when sat by the fireside, relaxing, with Mac's arm around my waist, watching the young braves learning the tribal war dances. With their painted faces and gleaming oiled chests, they would holler and leap high in the air, all the while brandishing their weapons. I for one was frightened by their antics, but Mac would jump up and join them, causing me much laughter.

I was seeing Mac in a different way: back home his Scottish ancestry was always to the fore, but here in the Indian camp he became more Cree. Alone with me he was the same Mac that I'd always known, but I hardly recognized the man he became when mingling with his family.

He took on the personage of an Indian brave, joining in the boisterous pony racing, and then stripping off his shirt to wrestle in the dust with his friends. I fully realised for the first time what being a half-breed meant.

Our visit soon came to an end. The festivities would continue for another week or more, but we needed to return to the farm. We had been given a feast the night before we left, and I had been loaded down with gifts. I now possessed many pairs of beautiful handmade moccasins, and a delicately embroidered bag encrusted with blue beads that Chief Bear-Paw's wife had made for me.

I felt very touched by their friendliness and goodwill, and endorsed Mac's invitation to visit us whenever they liked. As we left, the tepee was being dismantled, and soon Mac's cousin came running after us to load it on the wagon. It was ours to use as we wished. I was pleased, having enjoyed my stay inside its calming interior, and envisaged some romantic evenings looking at the stars on our own land.

We were now eager to reach home and wasted no time on the journey back. The Williamson's boy had managed well in our absence, and he was delighted with the fringed buckskin jacket that Mac had purchased for him, and I sent moccasins for his mother and sisters. As he rode away, Mac and I stood at the yard gate to wave goodbye.

It seemed very quiet, the stillness and hushed air of the prairies contrasted strangely with the noise and bustle that we had left behind in the Indian camp. Mac took me in his arms and said he was glad to be back home again, and I too was glad – relieved to be home, but glad that I had my Scottish Mac back once more.

The Indian Camp, and the McKenzie Place. 5th of July 1912.

A Latvian Wedding

As winter reached its peak, we were virtually stranded on the farm. The heavy snow storms, that had at times drifted as high as the cabin's roof, had now ceased, and freezing arctic winds had frozen the drifts solid. It was quite a stirring sight, with a white wasteland stretching as far as the eye could see. It reminded me of the frosted icing my mother would spread on her Christmas cakes.

We were cocooned in our cabin with the wood stove's smoke roaring up the chimney pipe. Mac had forced a path to the barn, and twice a day slid along it to feed the livestock, and milk the cow. The veranda was piled high with wood which he fed from the store whilst he was out. He would come back in to the cabin with his eyebrows white with frost. It was a strange peaceful time, and at its coldest we kept to our bed for much of the day. It was good that we were such a convivial couple who always found our greatest pleasure in each other's company.

I had forgotten how bitter cold the prairie winters were, and the isolation that surrounded you for months on end. Any socialising with the neighbours had finished with the first snow storms, and so early one morning we were surprised to hear footsteps crunching on the steps. It was the Williamsons' farm lad, come with a message from Grace to invite us to a wedding the following week, to be held up river at Cook's Creek. The lad had reached us with Owen Williamson's sleigh which was harnessed to a team of horses who had pulled him along the track. He was frozen to the marrow, so whilst Mac saw to the team I took the lad inside to warm himself by the stove. I was enthralled by his mode of travel, having heard of people travelling this way but had not known that the Williamsons had a sleigh.

Grace's note excited me even more: there was to be a Latvian wedding the following Sunday up at the creek, and all who could get there were invited. She explained that we could go across the frozen lake where the ice was at least two foot deep, a quick route, and quite safe until the thaw. This treat I was not prepared to miss. I didn't know the Latvian family, but was determined to be at their wedding. Mac too was glad of a diversion, and we sent the lad back after a hot bowl of broth to say we would be ready on the day.

Come Sunday we waited for the sound of the sleigh bells coming down the track. We had wrapped ourselves in our warmest clothes, and had tins of hot water nestled in beds of straw to put at our feet, plus a plentiful supply of furs to keep us snug. Mac had crossed rivers and lakes in this fashion many times before, but it was a new and exhilarating experience for me. I was happy to see Grace again after our long hibernation during the worst of the snow. She didn't know the wedding hosts either, having heard of the invitation when going by sleigh to the store.

It was thrilling to skim across the wide lake, the horses' feet muffled to prevent them slipping. And fortunately the sleigh was a large one, big enough to hold the Williamson family as well as Mac and I. I was elated by the journey, an adventure I had never thought to have.

In no time at all we were at Cook Creek, which would have been at least an hour's journey overland. Owen coaxed the horses up the frozen bank and we took the track to the wedding venue. The sound of loud music led us directly to the farmhouse, a weathered timbered building much larger than the usual cabin. The other guests poured out to greet us, and their cheerful appearance showed signs of them having drunk the health of the prospective bride and groom many times over. The family from Latvia consisted of three brothers, their wives, and a large brood of children, which explained the large house, but even so it must have been a squash to fit them all in.

They were a charming family who made us strangers very welcome. It was a daughter that was getting married, her groom newly arrived from Latvia and with not a word of English. She was a pretty girl, or as Grace whispered, still a child, not looking a day over fourteen. But perhaps, as I suggested, that was the way of things in their country.

The ceremony was performed by a heavily bearded man dressed in rich embroidered robes, and the bride and groom were in their national costume, altogether a very colourful wedding. Tables were laden down with a great variety of food, many that I had never tried before, and I enjoyed the pickled dishes immensely, but found some of the spicy food hard to digest. Later the floor was cleared for dancing, and after half an hour or so I had to beg for a rest, as the Latvian style of dancing was very energetic. As I was swinging around the room on the arm of an elderly gentleman I could see Mac being equally propelled by a very large lady. It was all extremely good fun, and I wouldn't have missed a minute of it.

We left before sunset, as Owen wanted to be across the lake before dark. This was an early end to a wedding by prairie custom, and we could still hear sounds of merriment as we drove away, and I'm quite sure the Latvians would be celebrating until dawn. It had been a most unusual day and a welcome diversion to winter's isolation, and I was determined that before next winter Mac and I would have our own sleigh.

But the delights of the day were not yet finished. As we glided across the lake the sun was setting, and we were treated to the most glorious sunset I had ever seen. The sky was a mass of scintillating colours which were reflected on the icy surface of the lake. It was truly a transfixing sight, and the only heavenly comparison that I had seen was in the fall after we had newly arrived in Alberta, when Mac had called me outside to witness the northern lights which were said to be a reflection from the icebergs. I had been fascinated to see something I had only ever read about: it was as if heavy curtains had descended from the heavens, and hung between earth and sky with changing lights of mist.

Cuddled with Mac under the furs as Owen Williamson steered us over the lake, I reflected on my good fortune to see such wondrous sights.

The McKenzie Place. 27th of January 1913.

A Double Blessing

For the past few years we have had a good relationship with all of our close neighbours. The barn raising had helped clear up any misunderstandings there had been regarding Mac's origins, and if there had been some prejudice against him, Mac's own natural decency and courtesy to his fellow man had quickly dispelled it. We had been accepted into the tight-knit prairie circle, and enjoyed the social life that we all contributed to.

This neighbourhood harmony is very important when living in such a widespread isolated area. You never knew when you might need their assistance, or they yours. We had no doctor in the community, the nearest being in a small rural township a good six miles away. Fortunately most ailments could be cured by farming remedies. My father always vowed that what cured his cattle would work for humans too.

Mac's Cree grandma had been skilled in the use of wild roots and herbs. His Indian ancestors had survived for generations in this country before the white man's medicine came. Mac would collect plants and berries, and brew them up as an antidote for most minor ills, and could also if necessary set a broken bone.

The only close neighbours we saw very little of were a couple who lived on the northern boundary of our land. They had only recently moved on to the empty homestead, and were new immigrants, from Russia I believe. He a tall brooding middle aged man, his wife a much younger dark haired beauty, who seemed very shy. He spoke a little broken English, but she none at all. Mac and I had visited them when they first took over the farm; we were pleased that it was to be occupied at last. It had been deserted for over two years after its tenants had given up trying to scratch a living from it, and the land had gone to seed, which with the strong prairie winds was not good for the adjacent land that was ours.

The newcomers' cabin was decrepit, and needed a lot of work to make it more habitable before winter set in. Mac offered to lend any tools they might need, and volunteered his services too, but Mr Cheski, which was my translation of his name, shook his head and said no help was needed. I felt sorry for his young wife, unable to communicate and so far from family and home. Despite other neighbours offering their friendship, and giving numerous invitations, they never attended any parties or social gatherings.

I did attempt to visit them in the week before Christmas. I struggled through the snow to reach their homestead, and despite smoke curling from their chimney pipe the door was firmly shut, and no one responded to my knocking. I had thought of inviting them for Christmas dinner, not liking to think of the young girl being lonely at the festive season.

It had been months with no sight of them, although Mac had noticed that their fields had been recently ploughed. But it was a surprise a few weeks later to be woken in the early hours by the Russian's urgent banging on the door. He was quite distraught and grabbed me by the arm as if to pull me out of the cabin, and from what little we understood of his garbled speech and frantic gestures we deduced that he wanted me to go with him back to his farm. Presuming some misfortune had happened to his wife I hastily dressed and followed him out to his wagon, and with Mac riding close behind we sped to his homestead.

I could hear loud moans as I clambered up the rickety steps to their cabin, and felt some panic as to what I might find behind the closed door.

In the dimness of the room I made out the slight figure of his wife lying on the bed, but one look at her swollen stomach and I knew what the problem was. She was well advanced in labour, and the poor girl was terrified, as she might well be, set to give birth alone. I felt some anger against Mr Cheski that he had allowed this poor child to go through her pregnancy without a woman to talk to or offer any advice. Pride was all very well, but I considered he'd gone too far. Had he thought she would deliver it on her own with him out in the fields? I had no idea how these things were done in Russia, but it was not the way here.

She at least was happy to see me, and such was her relief she started to weep. I took her in my arms and wiped the tears away, telling her that all would be well. She didn't understand a word I said, but seemed comforted by my presence. Turning to her husband I curtly told him to fetch some water to put to boil on the stove; he seemed bemused by the whole affair as if he'd had no part in the making of it. Fortunately Mac showed him what to do and sent him out to the pump. I had helped at confinements before, but had never delivered a baby entirely on my own, except of course when giving birth by myself to baby William many years ago.

I made my name known to the girl by pointing to my chest and repeating it over and over again. She understood, and smiled, saying she was Petra. I kissed her cheek, and repeated her name, and she smiled at my pronouncement of it, but understood by my mime that I intended to stay by her side, and smiled her gratitude. Mac said he would ride to the Williamson's place and fetch Grace to come and help, which I thought a good idea as two pair of hands would be better than one, and Grace's calm manner would benefit us all. He kissed me and rode off in their direction to hopefully find them at home. The husband came back in with the pails of water and put them to boil on the stove, and then thankfully he disappeared out into the yard.

Petra's pains were more frequent and she cried out for her mother, talking wildly in her own language. I felt so inadequate in not being able to comfort her, but held her hand, and constantly wiped her brow, hoping that the baby would wait until I had some help with the birthing. I prayed it would be a normal one, and not come feet first as one of my old friend Mary McDonald's had done.

I left her for a minute to take the boiling pans off the stove, and to get her some water to sip. A sharp scream caused me to rush back to her side, she was arching her back with the pain, and her teeth bared in agony. This baby was in a hurry and I feared was not going to wait for Grace's arrival. I washed my hands and laid out a clean towel ready to catch it in.

From the sodden sheet she was lying on I presumed her waters had broken some time ago. It was so frustrating to not be able to converse with her, there being only so much you can cover by mime. Between the frequent labour pains she was enduring I managed to change her bed linen, noting the fine embroidered sheets that were in the chest she had pointed out to me. And anxious that she shouldn't soil them, I found some that were coarser and more worn, and obviously not from her wedding trousseau.

When the pain came again, each time seeming more fierce than before I felt sure that the baby was almost here, and then when a minute later she started to push, I prepared myself to catch it. Her small frame was shuddering with the effort, but at last I saw the baby's crown, and with one final push it was in my hands, loudly protesting at its sudden entrance into the world. It was the sweetest little girl with a mass of dark hair. I cut the cord with some scissors that I'd earlier found in Petra's sewing box, and tied it with the narrow ribbon I'd also discovered there.

And then wrapping the baby in the towel I placed her into her mother's waiting arms. Petra was crying with happiness, and so was I, although a little of mine was relief. I turned back to make sure that everything that needed to be shed had come, when to my shock I saw another crown, and Petra was pushing again, with all the strength that I marvelled she could still find. And then there was another one, a second little girl with the same mop of black curls. I admit to panicking a little, afraid they were going to keep coming, and I not having enough arms to catch them.

Thankfully it was just the two, and by the time Mac returned with Grace in tow, I had washed them both, changed their Mother's nightwear and bed linen, and the pair of them were at her breasts. Of their father there was no sign, but Mac said he'd seen him picking stones out in the fields, but having got his measure I hadn't expected any more of him. Whilst Mac went to tell him of his double fatherhood, Grace and I sat awhile and marvelled at the wonder of birth.

Mac came back without the new father, who much to my anger had stayed out in the fields to finish his stone picking, having first told Mac that he was disappointed in his wife, as he had wanted a son to help him work the farm. It was the only time in my life that I regretted having no other language, how I would have loved to speak Russian so that I could tell him exactly what I thought of him.

We couldn't leave the young girl and her babies to his callous ministrations, so Grace and I decided to share the lying-in time; we would come on alternate days to tend to them. I said that I would stay that first night to make sure that there was some food cooked, and to be certain that Petra had some sleep. And so between us we got the girl through her lying in, and made sure she would be able to manage the babies on her own.

She was a bright, quick-learning girl, who after only ten days in our company was already using some English, and fortunately she was a natural mother too. Mr Cheski totally ignored our presence whilst we were looking after his young wife, and seemed quite indifferent to his beautiful young daughters. But despite his rudeness, Grace and I were determined to visit her as often as we could. We were both touched that she wanted to give the girls our names, and to our surprise, despite her husband wanting Russian ones, she defied him and insisted on her choice.

Although we had broken the barrier, and Petra was eager to have company, her husband never socialised. Whenever I visited he would scowl and stalk away, and not return until I'd left.

But by the following fall they had gone, selling up and moving away as silently as they had come. Two bad crops had finished them, and once more the homestead stood empty and neglected. I had no idea where they went, hopefully for Petra's sake to a community of her own people, or even back to Russia. I missed her and the children, and wondered how the little identical twins would fare if in Russia and answering to the very English names of Grace and Edith.

The McKenzie Place, 5th of October 1913.

For King and Country

I knew what he had done as soon as I saw his face. Mac could never hide a secret from me; his guileless blue eyes always gave him away. He had done it whilst I was talking to our neighbour in the store. She had been telling me of her dismay that her two sons were talking of enlisting, and saying how lucky I was not to have that worry. She didn't know that Mac had been talking of nothing else for the last week or more. I had been almost driven insane by his constant talk of war and duty. I simply couldn't accept his reasoning. What did the war in Europe have to do with us? We were farmers, and more use to the Old Country with the plentiful crops we produced.

He had told me that morning that he felt he had to enlist; our neighbours, he said, were sending their sons, and in some cases their husbands too. But not you, I'd reproached. I couldn't accept that he owed his own country any allegiance, never mind England. I had angrily raised my voice and snapped back nastily that his country called him a half-breed, and he didn't even have a vote. He'd left the cabin without another word and walked his land, leaving me sat at the table, head in hands, weeping as if my heart would break.

We had driven to Red Deer in silence. Mac had tried to talk to me, but I had turned away. The uncomfortable quiet made the journey seem twice as long. I desperately wanted to hold him close and show him that he simply couldn't go and leave me. But foolish shrew that I was I did nothing, and the clip clop of the horses' hooves was the only sound between us. Behind my anger was fear, and the dread of losing him. I couldn't envisage my life without Mac being part of it.

He told me on our journey back to the farm that he'd enlisted, taking the oath whilst I had shopped. He had been told to report to the regimental headquarters in Edmonton in ten days' time. He was now officially a recruit in the Royal Canadian Artillery and after training would be shipped to Europe. "Yes," I bitterly retorted, "to become cannon fodder in a war that's nothing to do with us. You are half Indian, and it's not so long ago that your ancestors were fighting the British to survive."

Mac turned to me and nodded, "Don't you see, that's the reason I want to fight with the Canadian army, to show that I am an equal citizen and that my mother's people are worthy of being part of this nation." I took his hand in mine and held it to my face, showing my acceptance of his decision.

We had just ten days, why spoil it with recrimination? As the days sped by I learnt to dread every second of the clock's ticking, as each hour was taking us nearer to parting. However, I had reluctantly accepted his going, and understood his need to feel part of his country's contribution. I did my best to be cheerful, not wanting to mar these last few days. We talked of everything but the war, and his going. We reminisced, and he spoke of that first day he'd seen me, standing on the station platform pointing my rifle at his head. He said that even then he had fallen in love with me and knew that one day we would be together.

I admitted that despite him stinking to high heaven I'd also felt the attraction. I told him about my jealousy that he had gone to Black Rock to find a tart. He laughed, and said his sole reason for going there had been to have his choicest fur made into a stole for me, but admitted that he'd been disappointed when I'd said my man was out in the fields, and how relieved he'd been to find me a widow, thinking he said, that he might have had to make me one, so determined he'd been to wed me. We laughed and loved a lot, but in the whole ten days we never once referred to his going, concentrating on finishing the spring planting, both hoping he would be home again for the harvesting.

We drove back into Red Deer to stock up with provisions, enough to keep me going for the months ahead. Mac had arranged with Erich Seebach, our Dutch neighbour, to watch over the fields and I think also to keep an eye on me. Erich promised he would bring Annika, his recently wedded wife, to visit whenever possible, but as she spoke little English and I no Dutch, I felt our meeting might be a little strained. I think Mac would have preferred me to have moved into town whilst he was away, but I would not consider the idea. I had no intention of leaving the farm unoccupied, we had both worked hard to make it our home and I was not going to desert it now. I would be here always, and it was here that I would be waiting for his return.

That last day before he went was hard. We stayed close to each other, not wanting to talk, but just feeling the need to continually touch, and be as one. I wept in his arms as night fell, and he wept with me. But come morning I put on a brave face, not wanting to send him off with a memory of my sadness. He was to travel to Red Deer to meet other volunteers from the area, and then they would go on to Edmonton together.

All too soon morning came, he did his chores, and then sat with me until he could no longer delay his going. He had planned to ride as far as the Seebachs' place, from which Erich would drive him into town, and then, good neighbour that he was, he would stable Mac's horse until next time he came out with my post, when he would fasten him to the back of his wagon and bring him back home.

Mac saddled him and then stood by his side, the reins loose in his hands, and at a loss to know how best to leave me. But I tried to make it easier for him, and briskly jumped the porch steps to enfold him in a quick hug, and with one last peck on the cheek told him to go. We had said all there was to say the night before. He mounted his horse, dug his heels into its rump and sped off down the track, halting just a while at the gate to take a last long lingering look at his farm, and then with one last wave to me he turned and galloped away.

I stood dry eyed until I could see no further sight of him, and having waited until even his dust had settled, went back inside the cabin. And then, almost blinded by my tears, I saw his old jacket lying on the chair, lifting it, I could smell him in its folds, and feel the very shape of him as I cradled it in my arms. I sunk to the floor, and wept until I had no more grief to spare, and then I prayed as I had never had before, asking whatever god was listening to please bring Mac safely back to me. And then, I started the waiting.

The McKenzie Place. 10th of April 1915.

Good Neighbours

I knew he would come. Every day for the past year I'd anticipated such a visit, and when I saw the dust cloud rising in the distance I felt sure that this was the day. I went outside and sat on the wooden porch, straining my eyes as I tried to determine the identity of the lone rider. Despite the warmth of the midday sun I felt a sudden chill and took a shawl to drape around my shoulders. The only sound was my chair, rocking backwards and forwards, squeaking on the uneven floor boards.

The horseman was getting closer, and now I could hear the pounding of the horse's hoofs as he galloped down the dry rutted track that led to our place. I had little hope that it wouldn't be whom I was expecting; my loneliness had given me ample time to speculate on his coming.

I sat forward, staring intently, please God, let me be wrong – it could be a neighbour returning from a visit to the trading post, dropping off my mail and checking that all was well. I had been fortunate in my neighbours; they had helped me a great deal since I'd been left alone. Despite the long distances between homesteads, and their own heavy work load, they had filled our woodshed with enough chopped logs to see me through the coming winter, and had managed to give precious time to plough and sow our land last spring.

My years spent on the prairies had made me realise and appreciate the importance of having good neighbours. When hungry for company, a prairie woman would journey half a day just to share a coffee and have some feminine conversation, and whole families would travel fifty miles or more for a wedding party or funeral wake. A neighbour without hesitation would ride through the night to help deliver a baby, or tend a dying friend. I had learnt that it didn't do to shun people in the wilds. Your very life could depend on their kindness and support.

The man on horseback was almost at the gate, I turned away, clasping my hands together to stop them trembling, and closed my eyes, trying to blank out the thoughts that were running riot through my head. As he reached the porch I stood up, smoothing back my hair, and wetting my dry lips, desperately holding my breath to try and still the fastness of my beating heart. I smiled a greeting to him as he climbed the porch steps, my agitation only betrayed by the twisting of the gold band on my finger, and the silent twitch of my mouth.

"An urgent cable, ma'am," he said, touching his cap and lowering his gaze, seemingly unwilling to look me in the face.

"I know," I replied, "I've been expecting it." I reached for the flimsy envelope and carefully placed it unopened into my apron pocket, and then turned to him offering refreshments, and thanking him for making the long journey to bring it to me. I poured him coffee from the pot on the stove, cut him a slice of fresh baked bread, placed them by his side, and then I fled, running across the yard to the barn, where standing in the safety of its dimly lit interior I felt able to take the envelope from my pocket.

I held it for a long time, lacking the courage to open it, not wanting to face the reality of my fears. I thought of the few eagerly awaited letters that I had received since he had gone, of how I'd torn them open, so anxious to have news of him, reading them avidly until their scrawled lines had become so familiar I could recite them as I churned the butter or stood at my washtub, such humdrum chores made more pleasurable by repeating his loving words. Despite their infrequency they had kept me sane during the long repetitive days and lonely nights of his absence.

I abruptly cut short my drifting thoughts and tore the cable from the envelope, quickly skimming its contents before crumbling it up in my tightly clenched fist. I stared bleakly around the barn. He had built it himself when we had first taken the place, I had helped him stack the hay bales and he'd kissed me when we'd finished, telling me that I had the makings of a good prairie woman – and when he'd left I'd stood strong and competent like he thought I was, and he didn't see the tears I'd shed as he rode away.

I smoothed out the cable and read it again, the words dancing in front of my eyes: *'SORRY TO INFORM YOU > A BRAVE AND ABLE SOLDIER'* – I read no further, I had no need, I'd known for a long time. It must have happened when I had that sudden sharp intake of breath, and had felt the crushingly heavy weight in my chest, which had been followed by such a lowering of my spirits that I had been filled ever since with a deep despair – yes, I had known.

But he'd promised me he would come back. I suddenly screamed out his name, angrily repeating it louder and louder, the anguished sounds echoing around the high walls of the barn, and then I fell to the dirt floor, and at last I wept – knowing that soon the neighbours would come.

The McKenzie Place. 7th of June 1916.

Afterwards

I have only a vague recollection of the days that followed. My grief was totally consuming. The telegraph boy had found me in the barn, and, becoming unnerved by the intensity of my anguish, had mounted his horse and fled back to town to spread the news of my loss.

I had continued to lie on the barn's cool earthen floor, utterly stricken by the cable that was still tightly crumbled in my clenched hand. I could have been there for hours or days, being unaware of anything but the devastating news that I'd just had confirmed.

I became conscious of others kneeling by my side, and found myself lifted into the comforting arms of Grace Williamson. She and her husband Owen had left their chores and come immediately. They had heard the news. There was no one, other than my own kin, that I would rather have had by my side. Good people, who had welcomed us both into their home in the early days of our arrival here.

I allowed them to lead me back to the cabin, and whilst Owen saw to the animals, I had leant against Grace's soft bosom and silently wept. She'd soothed me like a child, and encouraged my tears. Soon others came, close neighbours, and those whose sons and husbands were still overseas, and who despite their own fears came to offer comfort and their regret for my loss.

Grace and Owen would have liked me to have gone back to their home to stay awhile, but I'd vehemently refused, aghast at the idea of leaving the one place where I could still feel Mac's presence. Grace insisted she would stay with me for a few days, and after Owen and the others had departed, she'd fed me bread and milk, and then tucked me up in bed like one of her children.

Surprisingly I'd slept, a quiet dreamless sleep from which I woke refreshed, and strangely calm. I'd felt more composed, and had quickly bathed my face and dressed, and while Grace still slept, went out and sat on the porch, where I'd watched the sun rise, and marvelled as ever at its beauty.

I'd felt anger that Mac couldn't share its glory, and that his blue eyes would never again look on the magnificence of a prairie sunrise or the splendour of its setting. I strongly felt his presence, and clearly had a vision of him, sitting next to me, leaning back in his chair, his long legs resting across my knees as we had so often sat, both tired from our chores, but content to be together.

But then the reality had come and I'd raged at his death, angrily beating my fists against the cabin's timbers. Grace had rushed out, still in her nightwear; greatly alarmed at my torment, she'd led me back inside, and quietened the deep gulping sobs that had shook my body.

There were times in the following days when I'd thought I had lost my reason. I repeatedly imagined Mac at my side, and often I would reach for the waistcoat he'd left hanging on the door peg. I would press it to my face, hungrily savouring its familiar aroma, taking comfort from it as I held it close, but also achingly grieving for the loving man who would never wear it again.

I'd told Grace to return home, she had a family to care for and a busy household to run. I'd greatly appreciated her loving concern, but I wanted to be alone, to come to terms with my loss in my own way. She reluctantly left, and I'd immediately felt more at peace within myself, and more free to mourn. Owen had insisted on sending his boy each day to attend to the livestock and other chores, and I was grateful for this attention, and for the many kindnesses shown me by all the neighbours.

Six weeks later and Erich called by with my post, which he had got into the habit of collecting from the store. A long awaited letter from my sister, a bundle of circulars, and a brown enveloped package that bore the distinctive stamp of the war office. I shared a coffee with Erich, hoping he wouldn't linger, as I wanted to open my mail, but only when I was alone. At last he left and I quickly scanned my sister's news: she had obviously not yet received my sad missive, as her letter was full of the war and the limitations it had placed on their lives. I then sorted through the circulars, still not finding the courage to open the package, dreading what it might contain.

I went out to sit on the porch and with trembling fingers tore off the wrapping. The contents took my breath and I gasped with the pain of seeing them. In my hands were Mac's gold tribal band, and the pocket watch that had been my wedding gift, that we had chosen together whilst on honeymoon in Vancouver. I closed my eyes and held both to my lips, trying to sense the very spirit of Mac within them, but could only feel the coldness of their metal against my face.

There was more in the package, a short note from an officer telling me what a sad loss to the regiment Mac had been, and what a brave and noble man he was. Alongside lay another envelope which stabbed me in the heart as I recognized Mac's handwriting on the cover. It was addressed to me, and when I carefully opened it I found a letter, dated the day of his death.

My tears are dampening the writing paper and I am afraid that they will blot out the precious words, so have sat a while longer, striving to compose myself until at last I feel strong enough to read his final letter.

France.

My Dear One.

I must be brief, we are preparing for tomorrow's early onslaught on the German trenches, and soon we must use the darkness of night to take the guns further up the line.

How can I write my feelings for you in such a short time allotted? You are my very staff of life. The love we share is the one true meaning that I give thanks for in every prayer. Your precious face is forever in my thoughts.

I think of you back home on the farm and it's the only moment of sanity that I have in this black hole of inhumanity. Every day I see the youth of Canada and England slaughtered on a whim of officialdom. There is no glory or pride in this war. You were right, my darling.

I long for you, and the open land of our homestead. I pray to the gods of my mother's people and also to yours, that amongst all this carnage I can survive to return to your loving arms.

But my darling, I might not. And I don't want you to grieve for me, only to think of me as I was. We might not be allowed to grow old together, but the love we have shared will keep us forever close. Wherever I might fall there will always be part of you with me, and I will be at peace knowing that I had fought for my country. If the worst should happen, sell the farm and move back west. I want to think of you with the old friends who love you. Don't mourn me, just remember the love we share. My dear one, I have to go, it's time to prepare the horses for their work.

Know that I'm not afraid, whatever my fate. I know that one day your Golden Eagle and his White Flying Bird will soar again together.

My heart is always yours – your loving husband, Mac. x x x
28th of May 1916.

I sat awhile, holding the precious letter in my hand. Strangely, no more tears came. I had been greatly comforted by his words, and felt closer to him than at any time since he'd left. After a while I reread his letter and then carefully folded it before placing it with the gold band and pocket watch into my jewellery box, turning the key. I knew I would not read it again. I was closing that part of my life, secure in the knowledge that one day, somewhere, we would soar together again.

The McKenzie Place. 15th of June 1916.

Another New Beginning

Once again, I found myself journeying to Blue River Halt. The very noise that the wheels of the train made as it sped along the track seemed to mock me. Three times I had made this journey, twice with hope of a new beginning, but now for the first time in my life I had lost any expectation of a fulfilling or happy future. My passion for life had died with Mac, and I now felt an empty shell of the woman I used to be.

I had done as he asked – sold the farm, and was travelling west to the friends who I knew would welcome me with open arms. It had been difficult leaving the one place where I had felt close to him, but I knew that I couldn't realistically run the farm by myself, and couldn't expect our neighbours to do more than they had already been doing – their kindness and help had been above what anyone could ask of them.

The farm with stock and implements had been bought as a whole by a young Dutch couple only recently wed. Erich Seebach had driven them over to see the place, and he showed them round, as I was too despondent to be hospitable. To see the happy smiles on their faces, and their enthusiasm as they stood hand in hand surveying their purchase, was hard to endure.

The night before I left I'd sat out in the barn, silently saying goodbye to everything that was precious to me. I didn't sleep, but spent the night on the porch waiting for the sun to rise, and glorying in its splendour as it lit up the prairie in front of me – sadly, it would be the last time I would sit there and see it. But I was composed and dry eyed when Owen Williamson came to collect me, and drove away from the Homestead without a backward glance.

And now here I was on the train with just my wicker trunk as before. All I had left of Mac was his pocket watch and gold wrist band, both of which I kept close, these along with my silver locket were the most precious of my belongings. Underneath my winter coat I wore his old work waistcoat which he had hung on the bedroom door when he'd left. I kept it by me at all times, unable to wash or discard it, but taking comfort from the familiar image it gave me. I say that I had nothing left of our too few years together, but in fact I had wondrous memories of the time we'd shared, which had helped to keep me in sound mind these past months.

As the train neared its destination the reality of my future became more pressing. I had instinctively headed back to Blue River Halt, but with no thought given to my status. I didn't want to be one of those middle aged widows who drifted from friend to friend, dependent on their good nature for a home and sustenance. At no time did I ever consider leaving Canada; I had too many roots here now, and despite my two sons being in England I had no desire to go back there. I was too used to my independence to wish myself back under my brother's guidance, and I had the funds from the farm sale to support me in whatever venture I undertook. But for now I needed the wise counsel and loving support of my dearest friend who would be waiting for me at the end of my journey.

As the train pulled into the station and the conductor called out, "Blue River Halt, anyone for Blue River?" I had a brief recall of past journeys, but quickly put those memories aside when I saw Mary McDonald peering anxiously at the disembarking passengers. I waved and called her name, and was soon engulfed in her warm embrace. We shared happy tears, and then took stock of each other – she had become as round as she was tall, but still retained a merry twinkle in her eyes, and the cheerful smile that always made me feel warm and welcome. She scolded me for being so thin and said her aim was to fatten me up a little, and then arm in arm we went out to the road where her eldest son was waiting with the horse and wagon.

The brief glimpse I had of the Station House showed little change, although Mary said there would be no one left whom I would remember. Agnes had gone to live with her sister in Vancouver, and old Sam had passed away last fall. It was now being run by a French couple, who if gossip were true were living in sin, and had let the place deteriorate shamefully. It felt so good to be with my friend again, and to listen to her often scandalous talk, which was never malicious but always amusing.

As we drove out of Blue River Halt I was astounded by the many changes that had taken place since I was last there. A busy thoroughfare now led to the station, two prosperous looking hotels fronted the paved road, and most surprising of all were the automobiles that lined the sidewalk. Mary said the cattle markets had brought more business to the Halt, and it was now well on its way to being a boom town. This was evident by the ladies' gown shop we passed, and even a picture house was advertising its nightly showing. I found it quite bewildering: my recollections were of a few shacks, a trading post, and a dusty track that petered out onto the prairie.

My stay with the McDonalds was exactly what I needed. The warmth of their family life and the companionship of my friend was the solace I had yearned for. James as ever was discreet and asked no questions of me but offered his usual cordial friendship. The children had become adults with the eldest two married and already making grandparents of James and Mary. My two boys were of a similar age, and despite recent photographs I couldn't envisage them as gangling young men like the ones around me. My hopes were still high that they would come out to Canada to visit me, but in truth, I often wondered that after all these years apart would we be compatible.

Time quickly passed as I enjoyed the warmth of their hospitality, and I was surprised to find that Christmas was almost upon us. I had been with them for nearly three months, and had become too comfortable. With rest, good food and sympathetic companionship, I felt restored to sanity. My thoughts were never far from my loss, but I was learning to take an interest in life again. I would never be able to express the gratitude I felt to the McDonald family for allowing me the space and time to grieve.

However I felt it was now time to plan my future, and despite their objections I was determined to move on in the New Year. I had it in mind to buy a house and to let rooms to respectable folk, thus putting a roof over my head and providing me with an income. I wrote to land agents, and auction houses, letting it be known that I was looking to buy a suitable property. I felt happy with my plan, well aware that I didn't have the right temperament to be an employee; I had spent too long in the freedom of the prairies to do justice to a confined position.

Before long I was receiving dozens of offers of empty houses, and Mary and I spent many hours debating the suitability of each of them. She obviously wanted me to take something in the area and remain close by, but most of the properties were scattered around the provinces, and only one seemed the most favourable to me – a newly erected three-storey house, with six bedrooms and a large garden suitable for cultivation. The price was within my means, and it had the added bonus of already being used as a rooming house. But to my friend's dismay it was situated in a small logging town north of Vancouver.

Mary tried her hardest to influence my decision, but despite my affection for her I was determined to make a new start elsewhere. I had happy memories of Vancouver, having spent my honeymoon there with Mac, and I felt the need to start this new venture in a place that I could feel comfortable in. I knew it was time to turn my back on the prairies and start afresh.

I departed from Blue River Halt on the 2nd of January. A few tears were shed as I waved the McDonalds goodbye, and a firm promise made that I would return if the property was not to my satisfaction. But as the train steamed its way towards the Rockies I knew that I would never live back there again. And for the first time since losing Mac I felt a surge of anticipation, and excitement for my new life ahead.

The Canadian Pacific Railroad. 2nd of January 1917.

More of Grandma's Journal

Black Ridge Gap

I arrived in Vancouver early afternoon, taking a room in a small lodging house near the centre of town. It was clean and reasonably priced, having been recommended to me by a kindly lady I had struck up acquaintance with on the journey here. She was travelling from Calgary to help out her only daughter who had just given birth to twins. She marvelled at my boldness, or, as she indicated, the foolishness I was undertaking. Best marry again my dear, she advised.

In truth now that I'd arrived I was also feeling a little doubtful about the unknown future that I had planned. But, after making myself presentable, I ventured out into the busy thoroughfare. After the quiet and slow pace of life on the prairies, I found the noisy crowds and bustle of Vancouver to be rather intimidating. On my previous visit I'd had Mac's protective arm to lean on, but now I was jostled on the busy sidewalk, and found it most disagreeable.

Taking a deep breath and straightening my hat, I plunged into the fast moving horde, and found my voice enough to inquire of a newspaper seller the directions of the agent, to whom I had written to expect me on this date. At last, after taking numerous false turnings, I found the office I was seeking, in fact it was but a stone's throw from my lodging house.

Strange that I could drive blindfold across the prairies, but feel so disoriented in the city. The agent was middle aged and most cordial. We arranged that he would collect me from my lodgings early the next morning, and then travel together to Black Ridge Gap to view the property that I was interested in.

With no inclination to explore Vancouver alone, I returned to the lodging house, ate a solitary supper and retired early to my room. That night I cried myself to sleep; my stay here had evoked too many memories of Mac, and the happy honeymoon we had enjoyed.

Come morning and anticipating a long day I had breakfasted early, and was waiting at the gate for the agent's arrival, feeling anxious, but having a premonition that the viewing would be successful. I was quite shocked to see him arrive in an automobile, although Vancouver's streets were lined with them. I, with my country ways, had been expecting a wagon and team. It was to be my first ride in such a vehicle, and when I had got over my initial fears I found it a very comfortable form of travel.

Once we had left the city behind we followed the river for at least an hour or more. I was amazed to see the mass of timber that was floating downstream, in parts it was so dense as to hide the water from view, and I felt I could have walked across them to the other side. Mr Tracey, the agent, said that they were coming down from Black Ridge Gap, which was our destination. The fast-flowing river transported them to the saw mills in the city. I was most impressed, having heard tales of their river passage, but never expecting to see such a sight.

The road ahead was gradually petering out to become a solid soil baked track, which in summer would have left a trail of dust behind us, but was now covered by the first sprinkling of winter's snow. We stopped awhile to allow Mr Tracey time to attach chains to the wheels of his automobile. "We can't afford to slip on these mountain roads," he told me. I began to feel a little less secure in his comfy carriage, especially as the track had become steeper and the vehicle was labouring as we started to climb up the twisting mountain side. From the window I could see the sheer drop down to the river below, and whilst appreciating the outstanding beauty of the scene, I admit I was finding it a mite scary.

After the huge open expanse of the prairies I was thinking these forest-lined mountains a little daunting. We passed frequent narrow logging tracks that seemed to disappear into an inky blackness without any ending. We had been travelling for most of the morning, and as yet I had seen no houses or any sign of habitation. In answer to my query Mr Tracey replied that the property we were to view was a little isolated, but had regular custom from the logging camp personnel, and he assured me that there were other women living in the vicinity, the wives and children of the loggers who lived in cabins deep in the forest. It was quite a community, he said, with their own schoolroom, and a well-stocked general store.

I was still not convinced that I was going to find the place I had visualised when reading the written details back in Blue River Halt. The remoteness was not a problem – I liked it, but I wondered what I could make of my life here in these silent brooding mountains. A few more miles and then we suddenly came upon a large clearing on the edge of the forest. The winter sun rays were beaming across it as if they had long been searching for a gap amongst the trees. Mr Tracey drove into the opening and turned to say we had at last arrived: this was Pine Valley House.

At the furthest end of the clearing was a three storey timber house, its natural pine wood reflecting happily with the snow-capped greenery around it. I got out of the automobile and inhaled the clear mountain air, and such was its heady power that I felt I was breathing properly for the first time in my life. I didn't need to look any further, I simply knew that this was where I wanted to live for ever. I felt as if this magical place had been just waiting for me to arrive and claim it. If only Mac could have shared it too, I was sure that he would have instantly fallen in love with it as I had done.

As I walked across the snow covered ground I heard a faint swishing noise in the distance, and crossing to the far boundary fence I was able to look down on to the magnificent valley below, and even see the river in the far distance. It was a spectacular view, and by leaning over I could just make out a teeming waterfall that cascaded down the mountain to feed the same river. This accounted for the swishing sound I could hear, and I found it immensely soothing. All around me was the pungent smell of pine, and the savour of fresh sawdust that floated through the trees from the nearby logging camp.

All this in my eyes was perfection, and I had already made my decision.

Vancouver. 4th January 1917.

Pine Valley House

Exactly one week later, I moved in. In a whirlwind of just seven days I had bought a house, shopped for supplies, and had a further trip up to Black Ridge Gap to meet my lodgers. I'd hardly had time to question my judgement or to feel any doubts about such a hasty decision. All I knew for certain was that, for the first time since Mac's death, I felt my life had some purpose again.

Mr Tracey had taken me to meet the owners, who were now living in a small cottage on the outskirts of Vancouver. They were two spinster sisters who had previously spent all their life in the mountains, but now ill health had brought them down to the city where medical care was more available.

They had decided to take boarders at Pine Valley House after their brother was killed in an accident at the logging camp. He had been the breadwinner for them all after their parents' deaths, and it was he who had designed and constructed the spacious house. I took a liking to them both and was disinclined to haggle over the asking price, but they themselves offered me a reduction, saying that I was precisely the sort of person they had envisaged, and would be always in my debt if I agreed to take over the house and its lodgers. So within a matter of days the house on the mountain was mine.

An employee of Mr Tracey had taken me up to have my second look around. It also gave me the opportunity to check the furnishings and household equipment. Everything was in good repair, although the general cleanliness of the place left much to be desired. I met the woman from the logging camp who was acting as a daily caretaker, cooking and cleaning for the five male lodgers, who were at present the only occupants. I met them only fleetingly as my escort was anxious to make our return journey before darkness fell. They seemed decent men, all eager to assure me of their respectability – on this point I decided I would reserve judgement until getting to know them better.

The day I moved in I hired a local carrier to take myself and all my numerous purchases up the mountainside to my new home. I was now getting familiar with the long tortuous climb up the winding track, and no longer felt a stranger in the midst of these towering forests. When the driver turned into the clearing I'd had such a feeling of contentment and peace that I was quite reassured that my previous perceptions had been correct.

Being still early in the day I wasted no time in unpacking, as I wanted the whole house cleaned before arranging my belongings. Maggie Watson, the temporary housekeeper, was preparing the lodgers' dinner in the large kitchen at the back of the house. I bade her to continue for today, but told her that I would be doing the housekeeping in the future. Not being a civil person she tore off her apron, threw it to the floor and stormed out of the house.

I had no regrets at her leaving so abruptly, but had not wanted to cause ill feeling on my first day in such a small community. However I quickly donned the apron, and in a whirlwind of activity finished the dinner preparations, scrubbed the pine dining table, and washed all the downstairs floors. I had not felt so alive and active in a long time, the crisp mountain air combined with my fast running adrenaline was working wonders, and the house already looked more cared for, and had a sweeter smell. The upstairs I decided to leave for the following day, as by my reckoning the loggers would soon be returning for their dinner.

I met them at the door, and after wishing them all good-evening, requested that they remove their boots and leave them in the porch. I informed them that a meal would be on the table in ten minutes, giving them plenty of time to wash-up in the outhouse where I had already placed soap and towels for their use. I could have laughed at the astonished looks on their faces, but kept my dignity, and turned and went back indoors, closing the door firmly behind me.

On my previous visit I had noticed them sit down at the dining table with soiled hands and the sweat of their day's work still on their brow. By the time I was ready to serve the stew, and some hot biscuits straight from the oven, they were all seated rather sheepishly at the newly scrubbed table, all with clean hands and their hair still damp from the pump. I gave them time to eat and enjoy their meal, and then after bringing in the coffee pot I said I would like to have their attention whilst I discussed the house rules I intended to have in my establishment. Again I was close to smiling, as the two youngest of my boarders stared back at me like two frightened rabbits at a stoat.

First I properly introduced myself, saying I was Mrs James McKenzie, but they could call me Mrs Mac. I promised the rules would be few, but were intended to be kept, and if they were infringed I wouldn't hesitate to terminate their stay in my house. At this I swear the youngest one gave a gasp of fear. But not giving any mercy I commenced to relate my rules – firstly no smoking in their rooms, and definitely no alcohol. I would insist that they all have a weekly all-over wash and also change their underclothes regularly, when mentioning the latter I noticed they all blushed a fiery red. Lastly, I emphasised most decidedly that no women were to be brought back to the house – this time just two of them blushed. In return, I said I would feed them well, and they would have clean beds to sleep in, freshly laundered clothes, and a respectable home to live in. "However, if none of this is to your liking," I very firmly told them, "you may pack your bags and leave right now." After I had finished talking a long silence prevailed, I searched the five faces before me, some whiskered and lined, and the two youngsters whom I could see that as yet had no need of a razor.

I sat back in my chair and waited for some response, at last the older man at the head of the table broke the silence. He was clean-cut and handsome-featured, and introduced himself as Billie Ward, the foreman of the logging gang. He said he would answer for all of them by accepting my rules, and gladly so as the last few months had been hell – "Begging your pardon, Ma'am," he quickly added. He went on to explain that after the two sisters had left, Maggie had come up from the camp to cook and clean for them. She had pocketed the money left for her services, but had done as little as possible. They had been buying food from the general store to supplement her cooking, and their bed linen and personal laundry had not seen a washtub tor many weeks – at this confession I made a mental note of tomorrow's most urgent job.

The two youngsters were introduced as Richard and Eddie, both now more reassured, having seen me smile and realising that I was not the ogre they had first thought. The quiet man on my left was Chalky White, who rarely spoke, but when he did his strong Liverpool accent gave away his roots. The fifth boarder was a giant of a man who took my hand gently in his as if he feared to damage it; he was Phillipe Simeon, a French Canadian from Quebec. In all they seemed a decent group of men, and I was satisfied they would give me no problems.

The next few months sped by so fast I could hardly believe that I had ever had a life elsewhere. It had been hard work cleaning up the house, and after inspecting the boarders' rooms, I'd suggested that they had a tidy up on their next free day. Chalky pulled a face and started to protest but Billie quickly silenced him with a ferocious look. The two youngsters had dug the garden for me, and much to their delight I'd rewarded them with a tray of treacle toffee. I'd planted and seeded it, and was now hopeful of an abundant vegetable crop.

I had little free time, but when I did I was happy to sit in my favourite place which was a window seat on the south side of the house. Its casement window overlooked the wooded valley below, and on a clear day I could even see the river twisting its way to the coast.

Some days, as I wrote to Mary, I feel like Snow White and her seven dwarfs, or in my case five. I would see them off to work after a good breakfast, standing at the door until they had disappeared into the forest, and then be waiting at night for their return. But, as I assured her in my letters, I was content and at peace with myself.

Pine Valley House. 2nd of May 1917.

A Logging Community

I found the Black Ridge Gap community very different from the prairie folk I was used to. The people in the logging camp seemed to be very suspicious of newcomers, particularly those who lived outside the camp like myself. There seemed to be a division of social rank, with the management personnel living further up the mountain in uniform wooden bungalows, whilst the workers and their families lived on the logging camp site itself. The unmarried loggers shared hostel accommodation or boarded privately, like my own five did.

I had been used to the open house hospitality of the prairies, but here invitations were more formal, and I felt I didn't quite fit into any of the required status. I was a lodging house proprietor thus making me not eligible to join the senior management's social activities. But neither did I fall into the category of the workers – and being a widow, I was not welcome in either group.

One Saturday evening, at my lodgers' request, I had attended the weekly dance which was held in the camp's mess hall. I loved to dance and my feet were soon tapping to the fiddler's tune, and I was disappointed not to have the opportunity to show off my dancing accomplishments.

The loggers crowded in the doorway drinking the local-made beverages, whilst the married women sat in a group sipping coffee and gossiping. Only the children were dancing and taking advantage of the music. There was one other lady who stood alone, but who occasionally allowed herself to be partnered by one of the prancing children. She smiled at me and shrugged her shoulders as if to say we were both suffering a lack of partners.

As the evening wore on the single men, fortified by the alcohol, became braver, and ventured to ask us to dance. Having accepted, we soon paid the price of being the subject of the gossiping women sat at the rear of the hall. However the pleasure of dancing outweighed any discomfort I might have felt, although quite often my partner's alcoholic fumes were not to my liking.

Whilst drinking lemonade and taking some fresh air between dances, I made acquaintance with the young woman who had been dancing with the children. She was the teacher at the camp's school, Martha Browne her name, and a sweet natured person she was. She had been in sole charge of the logging school for the past year. I found her a very congenial companion, and after our first introduction we met up as often as possible. I fell into the habit of walking down to the school house early evening after feeding my lodgers. We would sit together on the porch, enjoying a companionship that I had sorely missed since leaving Blue River Halt. She had been born in the province, but her late mother came from Derbyshire, and she delighted in the description I was able to give her of that beautiful English county that she had heard so much about, but never seen.

She would walk over to Pine Valley House on a Sunday and share dinner with us. I could see that my lodgers, and most of the camp's loggers, were all infatuated with her. She was a pretty girl with modest manners who was bound to have male admirers. However, she was lost to them, having been engaged for the last two years to a farmer's son from Ontario. He was a volunteer with the Royal Canadian artillery, and was at present somewhere in France. She confessed that she was feeling worried not having heard from him for a while. I comforted her, knowing full well those feelings of anxiety.

No one realised that I was a war widow, and I didn't enlighten them. I said that I had farmed on the prairies, but on my husband's death had decided to seek a new life. Gradually over the months that followed I began to be accepted by the rest of the logging camp community. Women would talk to me when shopping in the store, and when finding I had a talent for letter writing would beg my assistance with their correspondence. Twice a week I would join them at the camp to assist with the knitting of socks and gloves for our soldiers abroad.

As time passed I began to feel part of the tight-knit society, becoming used to the noise of the distant saws, and accepting the irritation of the fine sawdust that was always at your feet. The garden was flourishing and the house at last to my liking. My two young lodgers had left the camp's employment and moved back to Vancouver, there being very little entertainment in Black Ridge Gap for boys of their age. I'd become a mother figure to them, and for me they had been a substitute for my own two, so it was with sadness I saw them go.

A few days later Billie brought over two Ukrainian men who had only recently arrived in the camp. He said they were unhappy in the hostel, and would very much like to have lodgings with me. They were clean and tidy in appearance, and both to my surprise took my hand and kissed it, embarrassing me greatly. I was unsure about taking them, because although they spoke good English I was worried about their meals, having no knowledge of foreign cooking. They assured me that they would eat anything that I gave them, which I well understood, as the cook at the hostel was the same temporary housekeeper that had previously been here. So Carl and Stefan joined us, and I never regretted their coming, both always helpful and willing to help around the house.

The noise of the saws and the crash of falling timber was simply background noise here on the mountain, and you never really noticed it. But when a sudden silence prevailed your senses quickly became alert to its loss. Such was a day in late fall when I suddenly realised all was quiet, it usually signified an accident and I was worried for my lodgers and friends. Hastily grabbing a shawl I ran down the forest track, but before reaching the camp I could hear voices cheering, and excited chatter.

Martha hurried forward and excitedly told me that an armistice had been signed and the war in Europe was over. A wire informing him of the news had been received by the logging camp manager, and he had declared the rest of the day free from work.

My feelings were mixed: relief for my family in England who had suffered some deprivation from the hostilities, but a great sadness for the many like myself who had lost loved ones. The British Empire alone had lost three quarters of a million of young and able men, and the colonies could ill afford such a terrible loss.

Martha was dancing a jig around me, and I couldn't be sorrowful in her presence. She was so happy that her fiancé and all the other soldiers would soon be coming home. I hugged her, and softly so no one heard I whispered – "No, not all of them."

Pine Valley House. 12th of November 1918.

Martha

I had grown used to my friend Martha coming over for a visit after supper. It was pleasant on a summer's evening to sit out on the back porch sharing a pot of coffee, or in the winter to sit in front of the stove toasting our feet on the range. One of the lodgers would always walk her back after we'd had our fill of companionship.

Despite the difference in our age we had a lot in common, sharing a similar taste in literature and in our related values. She always urged me to talk about the old country, her maternal family having originally emigrated from there. She was fascinated by my description of the rural village that had been my home. And strangely enough she was as equally interested by my years spent on the prairie; although Canadian-born she had never left Vancouver until taking the school teacher's job here in Black Ridge Gap.

She was hoping to set a date for her wedding as soon as her fiancé returned, she'd heard that his regiment had already departed Europe and were homeward bound. Such talk was bittersweet, for although I was happy for her, I couldn't help reflect on my own situation, I would have given anything to have Mac on his way back to me.

We would often sit late waiting for my lodgers to return from the camp, and just occasionally her escort would show signs of being slightly inebriated, having overdone his refreshment. But Martha never had occasion to complain, her escorts always behaving impeccably. I imagine their fear of repercussions, if word should get back to me, was enough to keep them out of mischief. I had learnt to curb and have tight control over their exuberance, young men working and drinking hard, and with little feminine influence could have taken liberties.

I was helping Martha make her wedding dress; we spent many happy hours sewing the beautiful silk material that her brother had sent her from America. She had chosen a simple pattern but it had intricate smocking on the neckline which was testing our abilities. Whilst appreciating her happiness and excitement, I couldn't help but consider the loss I would feel when her fiancé claimed her. Naturally she would leave the Ridge school and move to Ontario with him, and I already could visualise the gap in my life that her absence would cause.

She was daily expecting word of his arrival, and could hardly contain her elation. Her classroom must have seemed very constricting when she wanted nothing more than to be in the vicinity of the general store where the long-awaited cable would arrive. The whole camp shared her expectations and it was the question that everyone greeted her with, all wanting to share in the popular teacher's jubilation.

My first knowledge of the coming of the long-awaited cable was the violent knocking at my door at breakfast time. It was Bessie the shopkeeper's wife, asking me to accompany her to Martha's cabin. She said the cable had come but it was bad news, and she thought it better if the two of us delivered it together.

I left my lodgers at their breakfast, snatched my shawl and hurriedly followed Bessie down the forest track, my mind racing, dreading our arrival, knowing the long awaited news would break the heart of my dearest friend. She was just leaving to open up the school room, and it was hard to witness the way her eyes lit up at sight of the shopkeeper's wife, and the cable in her hand. She looked puzzled at my presence but most likely thought I was there to share her happiness. She snatched the cable, and with trembling fingers opened it.

Her face went white as she re-read it repeatedly, and I stepped forward to catch her as she swayed a little, as if about to faint. I sent Bessie to put a notice at the school gate to tell the pupils that school would be closed until further notice, and then I led Martha back into the cabin and sat her gently into a chair. She was stunned, her face now blank with shock. I took her hands in mine and stroked them, all the while whispering to her that it was alright, I was there, and would stay as long as she wanted me to. I knew from experience that it was all she needed to know at that moment; tears and talk would come later when the trauma had lessoned.

Her fiancé had died aboard ship a few days before he'd been due to arrive in Canada. Such a tragedy for his loved ones, he had gone unscathed throughout the war but had succumbed to inflammation of his lungs on the day that his ship had entered home waters. The years of trench warfare, and exposure to the elements had weakened his chest, and lowered his resistance to illness. In fact he was a victim of war as much as if he'd died in battle.

I took Martha back to Pine Valley House and allowed her to grieve. My own heart was heavy, feeling her pain, yet knowing that she had to work through it herself. Two days later her father came to take her home, but she insisted that she wanted to stay on in Black Ridge Gap and complete her teaching contract.

She reopened the school the next day, and with her keen sense of professional duty was determined to continue to teach the camp's children for the remainder of the school year. But the Martha I had known had changed, thinner than before, with a gauntness about her that I realised mirrored my own. A ready smile no longer lit up her face, and her natural gaiety was subdued. Our friendship grew closer as we unconsciously shared our mourning.

Later she told me that her contract was due to expire in six months' time, and she had decided to join her brother in Texas, as she needed to make a new start away from Canada, and from all the memories of what might have been. It would be hard to see her go; we had developed a strong bond. She was the daughter I had lost, and I the mother she no longer had. I would greatly miss her, but I was glad that she was moving forward, and I was sure that her life would eventually come good. She was young, and hopefully she would find another fine young man to love her.

Black Ridge Gap. 18th of February 1919.

The Picture Show

Once a month we would have a picture show. It was a welcome diversion, and much appreciated by the folk in Black Ridge Gap. It was held in the timbered mess hall, which was one of the few amenities that the logging company provided for its workers. Everybody went: babies slept in their mother's arms, whilst children and adults alike sat memorised by the flickering pictures on the screen. Charlie Chaplin was the overall favourite, but any film was welcomed by our entertainment-starved community.

The film reels would arrive with the general store's delivery. And at some time during the day most residents would take the opportunity to visit the store to elicit the title of that night's picture show, although the knowledge was futile because we all attended anyway.

The night of the show I would prepare a light supper so that my lodgers and I could leave early to claim a seat in the mess hall. Even so on our arrival it was usually standing room only, however on this occasion I was lucky, as Martha, with great difficulty had saved me a seat on the front row. We usually had a film, and then had a break for coffee before watching a shorter documentary. Tonight we were fortunate as it was a Chaplin film which caused much merriment, the hearty laughter waking the sleeping babies much to their mother's annoyance.

The second film was a documentary celebrating the end of the war in Europe, and showed our soldier boys disembarking from troop carriers on their return to Canada. It was bittersweet for Martha and me, as we watched the harbour side lined with wives and girlfriends, all excitedly waving and blowing kisses to their returning menfolk. We took each other's hands, both consumed with thoughts of our personal loss, and what might have been. Such was my fantasy I found myself searching the face of each returning soldier, looking for that familiar one.

The film continued by showing scenes from the battlefront that our army had been involved in. It was disconcerting to go from the room's earlier laughter to see the terrible conditions that our men had endured. The trenches oozed with slimy mud, vermin sharing their sleeping quarters and the dead and dying their bed fellows. Mac had been lenient with the truth when he wrote that there was no glory or pride in such a war. I simply couldn't imagine how any man could come back from such a hell unscathed.

The camera moved amongst the troops, focusing on a group of men who were harnessing horses, preparing them to drag the big guns that lay alongside. And then unbelievingly, I saw Mac! He was holding a horse's bridle to steady him, and he looked directly into the camera, and smiled that slow dimpled smile of his. I screamed out, "It's Mac," and then for the second time in my life I fell forward in a dead faint.

I came round to find myself lying on the floor with Martha waving smelling salts under my nose, the lamps re-lit, and my five lodgers forming a protective circle around me to keep me safe from prying eyes. "It was Mac," I repeated, "it was my husband." I was totally stunned, and couldn't believe the wonder of it. To see my Mac again, after all this time of mourning, and the coincidence of him being in that one camera shot, which appeared in a film that I should be watching in this remote camp – unbelievable, if I hadn't just witnessed it.

Billie knelt down beside me, and said he had asked the projectionist to back track the film and show me that shot again. But first we would wait until everyone had gone and I could view it in private. I asked him and Martha to stay by my side, as I was trembling so much I couldn't hold the glass of water offered to me. Whilst the film was re-wound I went through a surfeit of emotions, both expectation and grief fought for supremacy.

The projectionist had found the reel and asked us to be seated. My gaze was transfixed on to that screen, my heart was beating fit to burst and my whole being cried out to the image which came alive in front of me. It was Mac, I had not been deluding myself. He looked tired, and haunted by the futility of the war he was fighting, but he smiled wearily as if he knew that one day I would be viewing it. I so wanted to reach across that chasm of time, and take him in my arms to soothe the hurt from his face.

The screen flickered into darkness, once more taking him from the light and my sight. Then the tears came, and I cried broken-hearted, like the time in the barn when I first had confirmation of his death. It was as if I'd lost him again. Billie discreetly withdrew, and left Martha and I to weep together.

We greatly comforted each other, and she insisted on returning with me to Pine Valley House. I readily agreed, grateful for her understanding and compassion. My five lodgers were waiting outside the mess hall, all looking uneasy, but determined to escort me home. I felt gratitude for the good friends I had made in this small community.

After a sleepless night with Mac in the forefront of my mind I came to the conclusion that I shouldn't be sad, but should rejoice that I'd had a chance to see his precious face once more before he died. It was a blessing that poor Martha hadn't had.

My sighting at the picture show had caused quite a stir. People marvelled that by the strangest chance I had seen my husband on film. A week later a newspaper reporter came up to Black Ridge Gap for the sole purpose of interviewing me about it, he took my photograph, and asked some personal questions which I refused to answer. However a few weeks later a copy of his newspaper found its way up the mountainside and was passed around the community, eventually reaching me by courtesy of my lodgers.

The headline of his story read: WIDOW WOMAN SPOTS DEAD HUSBAND IN BACKWATER FLICKS. I was at first annoyed at his brashness, but came to find it amusing, and was able to laugh at his journalistic liberty.

Pine Valley House. 6th of March 1919.

Tragedy at the Camp

A sudden silence was the first hint of tragedy. Noticeable, and unusual, as normally Sunday was the only day that the forest was allowed to revert to its natural stillness.

Living in such close proximity to the logging camp, your ears and senses became attuned to the whining of the saws, and the occasional hush, that was quickly followed by the resonant sound of crashing timber.

But the silence on this Wednesday morning was unusual, and I immediately felt alarmed and uneasy about its cause. The strange peace was suddenly broken by a strident blast of the camp's siren which was seldom heard, only used in an emergency or to summon workers to the camp. Only twice before had I heard its wail, once soon after my arrival in Black Ridge Gap, when tragically a logger had the misfortune to lose a leg in a sawing accident. And the second time I heard its jarring wail was for a joyful occasion, when it continually screeched to signal the end of the war.

I hastily grabbed my first aid box, and on impulse a bottle of whiskey that I kept in the house for medicinal purposes, and then I ran down the forest track to the camp. There was already a crowd of womenfolk gathered around the manager's office, anxiously asking for news, not daring to think of their loved one's vulnerability. The ground was wet from a heavy storm, and a logger's job made more dangerous by the soggy forest undergrowth.

The manager had no information other than to say there had been an incident a few miles up the track, and he was waiting for news too. We all stood silently by the office door, our eyes searching the darkness that was all we could see of the track as it disappeared into the dense forest. At last the sound of a heavy tractor could be heard in the distance, and soon its outline could be seen chugging towards the camp, black smoke pouring from its side as it laboured at top speed up the muddy incline.

There was a combined gasp of dismay when we saw that its trailer contained two bodies, both loosely covered by a tarpaulin sheet that did little to hide their outline. I felt foolish and inadequate, standing there in the rain holding my first aid box, and the bottle of emergency whiskey, knowing that the two men were past any such assistance.

Billie was driving the tractor, so I guessed that the dead men must have been part of his gang, and for the first time feared for my lodgers.

The manager came out and beckoned a young woman into his office; she had a baby in her arms and a toddler by her side. The look on her face when she came out was pitiful to see, friends and neighbours led her back to her home, and soon loud weeping could be heard through its thin timber walls. Billie came over to me, and in a choked voice and eyes clouded by tears told me that the other body belonged to Carl, my Ukranian lodger.

I was very shocked, unable to accept that the handsome and vibrant young man who only a few hours ago was sat at my breakfast table, was now lying dead on the trailer just a few feet away from me. Only last night he had been excitedly showing the photographs of his wife and children which had arrived in that days post. A quiet and hardworking man, who was saving every dollar he earned to buy tickets to bring his family to join him in Canada.

Billie took the bottle of whiskey from my hand and swigged it back, and for once I didn't say anything, and even though I was teetotal I too could have benefited from a swig. He explained that the two men had been working on a high pile of logs, fastening chains around them making the pile ready for moving down to the river. The rain had made them slippery and Carl had fallen, causing an avalanche of timber which had without any warning engulfed the two young men. The heavy logs had crushed them both, and despite the frantic efforts of Billie and his crew to rescue them they had died instantly.

It was a subdued suppertime back at Pine Valley House. Nobody had any appetite, and my heart went out to Stefan, he was devastated by the death of his fellow countryman. They had travelled out to Canada together and had become good friends. I took him to my sitting room where he could grieve in private, and later we talked of the arrangements we needed to make for a fitting funeral. The camp management were cabling Kiev to inform his family of the tragedy. I felt such pity for his young wife who would feel so far away and so helpless. Later we packed up Carl's belongings and discovered a tin box full of money, obviously his savings.

Stefan decided to travel back to the Ukraine to visit the widow and take her the cash in person. I felt very relieved as I had been worried how to get it to her. I knew Stefan was a decent man who could be trusted to safely deliver it, and who best to comfort her other than her husband's dearest friend?

We gave Carl a simple burial in the small forest clearing which had been designated as a cemetery for Black Ridge Gap. The only other graves were two small mounds, both the sad consequence of a recent outbreak of measles amongst the camp's children. The whole of the camp's population came to pay their respects, and we listened respectfully if without any understanding as Stefan gave a short speech in his own language. We all stayed on, as half an hour later the other young man who had died was also buried alongside. We had no clergyman, but Billie said the Lord's Prayer over them both.

Afterwards the men went back to the mess hall to raise a glass to the deceased, and I walked back home alone, feeling sorrow for all the brave young men, who had been robbed of their future whilst helping this wonderful emerging country of Canada prosper.

Pine Valley House. Black Ridge Gap. 10th of April 1919.

A Temporary Lodger

My front-facing bedroom had been vacant ever since Phillipe had finished his contract at the mill and returned to Quebec. I was happy for him, he had saved hard to realise his dream of opening a hardware store back in his home town, but I missed his reassuring presence; his size and daunting appearance had always prevented any escalation of arguments amongst my lodgers.

I was in no hurry to let his room, always relying on recommendations from the logging camp management or from my long-term lodgers. So it was quite out of character when I decided to offer the vacant room to a complete stranger.

He'd knocked on the door at an inconvenient time. I was busy baking, and had just put the dough to rise, with a dozen or more buns due out of the oven at any moment. I hastily wiped my hands and rubbed the smudge of flour off my nose before answering his knock.

The stranger standing there took me by surprise as I rarely had visitors at this time of day. He was smartly dressed, unusual in itself, for the camp and mill workers were not known for their dapper appearance. He raised his hat and said, "Excuse me, ma'am. I understand you might have a vacant room to let." Contrary to my usual caution I invited him into the sitting room and prepared to question him about his credentials, but at that moment realised the room was filling with smoke which was wafting in from the kitchen – the forgotten buns were burning. He followed me, and as I snatched them from the oven he quickly opened the windows and the backdoor. I turned to face him with stinging eyes and blackened buns, and saw the twinkle in his eyes and the twitching of his mouth, and realised that my own credibility as a competent housekeeper was in question. We both laughed, and that shared mirth made me instantly decide to take him as a new lodger; it had been such a long time since a man had shared any laughter with me.

He had come to the camp for two months to supervise a new cutting procedure and would normally have lodged at the camp hostel, but he said he preferred to spend his leisure time away from his workplace and had opted to live out. He introduced himself as Mike Windle, a native of Ireland, but resident in Canada since a schoolboy. Despite thirty years or so of living in the province he still had a trace of his Irish accent. He had a wife and two children, and lived in Calgary. He travelled all over the country, installing and overseeing the initial use of his company's machinery.

I introduced him to my other lodgers at suppertime. He had a mixed reception, all of my regular lodgers were timber men, and were not sure about an outsider in their midst. Normally a friendly group, they seemed ill at ease in his company, and Billie took me aside and asked if I was sure I had made the right decision, as he knew of other workers in the camp who would have been happy to have taken the front bedroom. I rather tartly replied, "Well considering that Phillipe's been gone for a fortnight or more, why didn't you say so before?" He looked a little shame-faced, and said no more.

My new lodger worked shorter hours than the timber men and he asked if he could return at dinnertime. I was in the habit of cooking a hot dinner in the evening when the men returned from work, making them sandwiches to eat at midday, as I preferred to have the house to myself during the weekdays. But I realised that it was probably difficult for him to find an appropriate place to eat, as he was not eligible to dine with the management and obviously not welcome with the workers. I agreed that he could come back and have his sandwiches in the dining room, taking into account that he was only here for two months.

So from then on he returned at 12pm each day and sat alone in solitary splendour at the big dining table. It was only a matter of days before he joined me on the back porch where I was used to eating my own midday snack. I found him good company and felt myself looking forward to the regular discussions we had. We shared a similar taste in music and I envied his talk of concerts that he had attended on his travels. We also had a mutual attachment to the prairies, he having lived for a time on a farm in Ontario.

It was so refreshing to have conversation with someone of a like mind, I realised I had been starved of companionship since coming to the Ridge. My lodgers were fine men, but I had nothing in common with them, my only other friend had been the school teacher, Martha, who was now in America. We were in regular correspondence, but it was not the same as the warmth of actual company sat on your porch.

He was a very gentle man, both in speech and conduct, and seemed to have an infinite understanding of my loneliness. Our chats on the porch became an important part of my day, and I resented the weekends when everybody was home for dinner. I talked of Mac, and he comforted me when the tears came. His first wife had died in childbirth, and he too knew the pain of loss.

In the weeks that followed we came to know more about each other's lives, and were amazed at our similarities. We were both from farming families, and like my first husband William, he and his older brother had travelled to Canada in search of land. And he had the same love and regards as I for this beautiful wild country that we had adopted.

He accompanied myself and the other lodgers to the monthly dance held at the camp, but unlike the majority of the loggers he didn't make for the drinking shed on arrival, but did his duty on the dance floor with the deserted wives. It felt strange being in his arms when he invited me to dance, his warm hand on my back was both reassuring and yet disturbing. I had danced with other men whilst attending the dances in the past, but none had made me feel so flustered and confused. He was a good dancer, light on his feet, and moving with a suppleness that his muscular body belied. I allowed myself to follow his steps, and to simply enjoy the feeling of freedom that dancing always gave me. It was only after we had danced half the night away that I noticed the whispering and gossip that the spectators were indulging in. Embarrassed I pulled away from him and with heightened colour left the shed to find some air.

Outside I took time to compose myself, and reflect on my discomfiture, realising that for the first time since losing Mac I had enjoyed being in another man's arms, and had felt happy to be there. Dismayed, I went to look in the drinks shed, searching for one of my lodgers to escort me home.

It was difficult serving breakfast the next morning. I deliberately didn't look at Mike, and fortunately it was the weekend so there was no shared dinner break. I stayed in the kitchen and scrubbed the floor despite the fact it had been done the day before, afterwards I took up my shawl and walked in the pine woods for a while. My head was spinning, the feelings I'd had whilst dancing felt disloyal to Mac's memory, but I couldn't deny that I'd had them. Sensing someone behind me I turned to find that Mike had followed me, which again threw me into confusion. He asked if he had offended me in any way, and trembling at his closeness I answered no.

Mindful of his marital status I tried to change the subject, asking him if he had seen the waterfall, and recommending he walk further on where he would get a perfect view. Foolishly I agreed to show him the way, well aware that we would be walking together deeper into the forest. I knew also that he felt an attraction to me, and that if I was sensible and not behaving like a giddy young girl I would be taking the path back home. But the needy part of me wanted to feel his arm around my waist again and to have his lips close to mine.

Fortunately prudence overtook my physical needs, and as we walked I talked of his wife and children, remarking on how much they must be missing him, and he them. Understanding my need for composure he also adopted a less intimate tone, and thus we completed our walk.

Three weeks later his job finished, he packed and prepared to return home. He was hitching a lift to Vancouver where he would then get the train to Calgary. I stood on the front porch waiting with him for the truck to come, he took my hand and thanked me for my hospitality, and leaned across to kiss my cheek, but almost as if by mistake he kissed me full on the lips. The kiss was sweet and passionate as I'd always known it would be, and I thought it just as well that the truck had turned the corner at that moment. We shared a look of regret for what might have been, then he picked up his bag and climbed into the passenger seat. I watched until the bend in the road took the truck from my sight, and he from my life.

That night I told Billie that his workmate could have the front spare bedroom.

Pine Valley House. 1st of May 1920.

Moving On

It had been almost five years since I had taken over Pine Valley House, and nearly six since I had lost my beloved Mac. Although I had made a new life for myself, I didn't feel content. Sometimes I felt as if the mountains surrounding Black Ridge Gap were closing in on me, squeezing the very breath out of my body, and I longed for the spacious vista of the prairies. There was an errant need in me for the open land that I had always loved, and the wonder of its vastness that had never failed to fascinate me.

My life in the mining camp was productive, I had many friends, and with a houseful of lodgers, a family of sorts. But I was no longer sure that my future lay here. I frequently suffered an inner loneliness which on occasion became overwhelming painful. At these times I sorely missed my boys and kin in the old country, although I knew I would never make that long journey back to Derbyshire.

I still called them my boys, but both were now grown men – Edward nearly twenty and already courting the village school mistress, and Thomas apprenticed to a local butcher. My brother, now disabled with arthritis, relied totally on Edward to run the farm, and thought of them both as his natural sons. Whilst ever grateful for his loving care, and the sure knowledge that both my sons would benefit from his will, I still had a slight feeling of resentment at his claiming of them. I'd always had hopes that one day they would come to seek me, and perhaps fall in love with this beautiful contrasting land, as I had done. Realistically I accepted that I had forfeited the right to demand such a sacrifice from them when I'd made the decision to come to Canada alone.

Since my friend Martha had left I had been restless, and felt strangely unfulfilled. People asked me why I didn't remarry, as widowhood was an unusual status in a country where women were in such short supply. I'd received many proposals, including one from Billie Ward, my long-term lodger. I had long been aware of his feelings for me, and had tried gently to dispel them. He was a good hardworking man, whom I knew would cherish and take good care of me, but I couldn't return his regard.

Just a few days short of reaching my 56th birthday I started to take stock of my life. I knew that no man could ever fill the place in my heart that had been entirely Mac's, but I was now resigned to my loss, and accepting that life had to go on. My discontentment stayed with me throughout the summer months, and after a sleepless night I came to the conclusion that I could no longer stay up here in the mountains, where I had come unwittingly to nurse my grief. In the early hours I made the decision to sell Pine Valley House and move on.

Convinced my resolution was the right one, I made plans that very morning to make tentative enquiries of the Vancouver agent who had been so helpful when I had been searching for my property. Without delay I wrote him a brief note and tipped one of the daily carters two dollars to deliver it for me when he arrived back in the city.

This done, I felt calm and quite buoyant, with a new found hope that my life could change for the better. To my amazement the carter brought me a reply on his return journey – a brief note to say that the estate agent planned to bring up a prospective buyer the following day.

I went into an immediate panic: I would have to clean the house top to bottom, and how would I explain the visit or its outcome to my lodgers? And it was such a small community that surely someone would notice their arrival, and rumours would soon abound.

I went into a frenzy of cleaning, and also denied the lodgers any supper until they had tidied their rooms to my liking. Billie took me aside to ask if I was feeling well, obviously concerned by my agitation. I told him what had happened, and how the estate agent's prompt action had thrown me into a turmoil. He cautioned against making any hasty decisions, and not wanting to upset him I promised to heed his advice, but all the while my head was buzzing with the excited thoughts of a new life awaiting me.

The agent's car pulled into the yard mid-afternoon and I opened the door to him and two middle aged ladies. He introduced them to me as Mrs Florence McAllister and her sister, a Miss Emily Tompson. Both were of Scottish birth but had been in Canada for a number of years. There was a Mr McAllister who was a semi-invalid, and it was for the sake of his lungs that had promoted their interest in moving up to the mountains.

A cup of tea and a couple of slices of fruit cake revived them from the long drive, and made them ready to inspect the house and garden. Both seemed pleasantly surprised by its decor and attractive position. I could remember my own delight at viewing it for the first time, and despite its familiarity I still found its locality attractive.

They questioned me closely about the lodgers, Mrs McAllister most anxiously inquiring of their morals, saying that as her sister was still unmarried she did have some concerns about the venture. I assured her that they were all gentlemen, crossing my fingers and hoping that they would have both left before the men returned home in their work attire, dirty and unshaven, although I had no qualms about my good recommendation, as all my lodgers were well-behaved, and I felt she need have no fears about her sister's virtue. I did have some misgivings about my lodgers' acceptance of them, as they did seem rather pious and with no sign of humour.

But I hardened my heart, and seeing their interest put forward the financial side of any possible transaction. Money didn't seem to be a problem, as seemingly Mr McAllister had run a successful business before his health had failed. Despite the sister's fussy ladylike manners, both were shrewd and business-like when a price was mentioned, and neither hesitated to bargain. I feared my lodgers could see an increase in their rents if these two determined ladies had their way.

After some yielding on all our parts an agreement was reached, and we shook hands to seal it. Since returning to Canada I had been surprised by my own business acumen, it would have been unheard of in my youth for a woman to conduct her own affairs.

I still couldn't believe that it was only forty eight hours ago that I had made the decision to sell, and now the deal was done. Mrs McAllister wanted to take possession in the fall, only two months away. I felt as if I was dreaming, but the deposit cheque in my hand was certainly real.

I had not even given thought as to where I would initially go, although I knew my ultimate destination would be the prairie. Despite my concerns about uprooting myself again I was happy to be moving on.

The difficult part was telling my lodgers; they had been with me a long time, and I had a good relationship with them all. I chose to wait until after supper when they were all relaxed on the veranda, mugs of tea to hand and tobacco packed into pipes, contentedly smoking and sharing the news of the day. Soon the drinkers amongst them would make their way down the forest track to quench their thirst in a different manner. I had never allowed alcohol in the house, and they had always respected my wishes.

In my nervousness I was perhaps a little abrupt in the telling of my decision, blurting out that as from the first week in September they would have a new landlady, in fact two.

A long silence was the aftermath of my outburst, all of them quite shocked. I saw a fleeting look of pain on Billie's face, and realised I had been lacking in courtesy not to have informed him first. I attempted to explain the need to move on with my life, but could see their lack of comprehension. I suppose it did seem strange that at my age I was envisaging a new beginning.

Soon of course the news was spread around the camp, and people were equally surprised at my sudden move. I spent a hectic few weeks packing my personal stuff, which I intended to place in storage until such a time I felt settled enough to claim it. Meantime I was planning to travel light.

On my last night I attended a party at the camp which was held in my honour. I was very touched by a pretty china framed travel clock that was presented to me by my lodgers, and Billie later gave me a hand carved wooden jewellery box that he had made himself, its highly polished lid useful for my reflection.

It was hard to say goodbye to Black Ridge Gap, and to all the friends I had there. But I wanted no fuss or long farewells. I cooked breakfast as usual on the morning I left and waved my lodgers off to work as normal, having a few special words with Billie, who I knew was upset by my going.

I prepared a cold evening meal guessing that Mrs McAllister and her sister would be too busy on their arrival to have time to cook. Taking off my apron and hanging it on the kitchen door for the last time made me realise what a big step I was taking, but ever optimistic I refused to have any regrets.

I was to travel back to Vancouver with the carter who was bringing the sisters and Mr McAllister up the mountain. It would be late when I reached the city and I intended to book into a hotel and stay a few days to take stock of my possible intentions.

I sat out on the back porch waiting for their arrival and taking a final look at the surrounding majestic mountains and their towering pine trees. I had been happy here, but always knew it had been only a healing and waiting time.

And later as the carter turned his wagon and we headed off down the mountain track I stared resolutely ahead, and didn't look back.

The Bay Guest House. Vancouver. 1st of September 1922.

Grandma's Last Journal

Cattle Country

When I left Black Ridge Gap I had no definite plan, or any idea of where I wanted to be; I simply recognised that it was time to move on. I needed to take stock of my life and put the many heartaches and regrets behind me.

My first need was to bank the large money order I had received for Pine Valley House, and then I decided I would have a little holiday, and perhaps a brief period of frivolity. Once I had safely deposited the money and taken advice on its best investment, I made for the large department store that must have only recently opened, never having seen it before on my previous visits to the city. Walking through the busy streets I couldn't fail to notice that my clothes were not up to fashion and looked decidedly shabby, and I resolved to do some shopping.

I was quite shocked by the prices; they had increased considerably since my last shopping venture. I had drawn out of the bank what seemed to me to be a very large amount of cash, although not according to the bank manager, who said I would quickly raise it on the payable interest due on my investments.

I had a most enjoyable morning, completely refurbishing my wardrobe. I felt a little guilty at being so extravagant, but reasoned I had worked hard for this treat, and so convinced myself I deserved it. I'd felt a little nervous when for the first time I wore a dress with the new shorter length, and although I thought myself a little fast to be showing my ankles in public I was delighted by the admiring glances I'd received whilst walking Vancouver's fashionable thoroughfares. To complete my spending spree I acquired two new hats, and some wonderful alligator skin court shoes with a matching handbag. Never before in my life had I been so unrestrained with money, but I had enjoyed every minute of my reckless spending.

The following day I looked up Agnes who was still living with her sister in West Vancouver. We had an emotional reunion – seeing her again had revived remembrance of the Station House, and of Blue River Halt. We talked of many things but neither broached or reminisced on the painful memories of people lost to us both. She was full of admiration for my fashionable clothes, but seemed surprised that I had not had my hair bobbed. Her own was shingled close to her scalp, and privately I thought it an ugly style, vowing never to have mine shorn.

After a week of such diversions I began to feel bored, recognising that I was not intended to be a lady of leisure, and afternoon tea parties, and even shopping soon palled. I was not yet ready to make a permanent decision, but had the notion of perhaps finding a temporary job. I made enquiries and was directed to a ladies' employment bureau where I was able to enrol, stating my preference for a rural housekeeping position. There was plenty of employment, but I rejected any idea of working for a single man, or the many unfortunate widowers with their brood of young children. Not very charitable of me, but I had particularly requested only a temporary vacancy, and had no desire to take the place of a wife and mother.

Within a day the agency had found what seemed a likely job, a farming couple were quite desperate for a housekeeper. The wife was recovering from a recent seizure and they needed help whilst she recuperated. The only snag was the location, they farmed in Alberta, and I had not intended to travel so far, and especially not to an area where Mac and I had lived.

But my boredom was reaching its peak, and I was reluctant to spend any more money on lodgings. So I accepted the position, my references were approved and by the weekend a rail ticket had been delivered. I was a little nervous about being employed by an unknown family, but reasoned that they too must be apprehensive about me. I left on an early train, somewhat dubious about the journey, as it would be taking me on some painful and familiar tracks.

Mr and Mrs Roache, my new employers, lived near Wainwright, a part of Alberta I knew well. I was to change trains in Calgary for the side line to Edmonton, and would be met at a rail halt called Yonker. Despite my anxieties I found myself enjoying the long journey, some spectacular scenery and a faster rate of travel than I had previously known. It was midnight when we reached Blue River Halt, and although I was curious to see its changes, I didn't leave the train. The Halt revived the sorrow I still carried from when I had first received the sad news of Mary McDonald's death. She had been a loyal and true friend, and had left us whilst still young, a victim of Consumption along with two of her younger children.

Yonkers was a small country halt, and I was relieved to see a shiny new truck waiting to collect me. Its driver, a grizzled stockman with the unmistakable posture of a prairie horseman, was a man of few words. He swung my bags into the back of the truck and gestured to me to climb in the front. Within what seemed a short distance we drove through gates that proclaimed us to be on Roache land. I asked my surly companion if we had far to go to the homestead, but he replied with a shrug, and a spitting out of a chewed tobacco wad, so I decided not to venture any more questions.

I could see that we were in cattle country: everywhere I looked there were prime herds grazing on the lush prairie grass, and the further we travelled I began to realise the true extent of the farm's acreage. And when at last we came in view of the house I fully comprehended the scope of the place I had come to work at. It was almost like a township in its own right, with a beautiful white-painted timber house at its centre, and at a distance the largest barn and granary I had ever seen, and by their side, extensive blocks of stockman's accommodation. They even had their own general store. I had heard of these large cattle ranches but had never expected to live on one.

Mr Roache came out to greet me, a big jovial man who shook my hand with a grip so tight my fingers whitened. He took me into a well-furnished parlour where his wife lay on the couch. She was a sweet faced lady whose seizure effects was still plain to see, her left arm lying stiff by her side and her speech impaired, but she smiled and bid me welcome. Her sister, who was temporarily looking after her, gave me a tour of the house, and explained that my duties would be mainly cooking for the family and making sure we had provisions in. They had their own butchery and grew their own vegetables, which along with the ranch shop made them totally self-sufficient.

The house was furnished with all the latest appliances: the large airy kitchen contained a modern cooking range, which I felt would be a pleasure to use. They even had an indoor water closet which was an undreamed of luxury. It really was a very comfortable job, I had a pleasant room at the back of the house with a large window overlooking acres of rolling grassy pastures, and my work was far from arduous. It was a new adventure, and one in very agreeable surroundings. I felt I was going to be content for the next few months, and would have plenty of time to consider my future.

The Roache Ranch. 22nd of September 1922.

An Unforeseen Romance

As well as the ranch being self-sufficient in its daily upkeep, it also made its own entertainment. Once a month Mr Roache would have the barn cleared for dancing, and would also provide a young steer for a barbecue. This event was popular, not just with his staff but with anyone within travelling distance, and a large crowd would attend.

I was looking forward to it, and to having the chance to wear one of my new gowns. My recent fashion spurge had not had much airing since coming to the ranch, being few special occasions to dress up for, although I had been able to pay a visit to my old neighbours, Grace and Owen Williamson. I'd overheard Mr Roache saying he was driving to Red Deer to collect some machinery, and I had begged a lift as he would be passing their homestead. Since my arrival three weeks past I had not taken any free time, so he was happy to drop me off there, and to collect me again the following day. We had a pleasant drive: the roads were rapidly improving, essential with all the increased traffic that now used them. Hard to remember the old dusty tracks that the horses and wagons used to journey on. Although, as we left the road to turn into the Williamson's place I noticed that the same old track still served them. It was the same track that led on to what had been Mac's farm, but this thought I firmly put away.

It was a happy reunion. I was very much in their debt for the help and kindness they gave me when I lost Mac. Without their compassionate aid I would have found it hard to manage, both the farm, and my grief. I noticed that the once-immaculate homestead looked a little rundown, and both seemed to have aged since we last met. I was truly sorry to hear that their only son Stanley had died, a victim of pneumonia, which he'd succumbed to after getting a soaking in the fields last fall. I could see that they were both ravaged by the tragedy, and it was yet another reminder of the harshness of life on the prairie.

On my return, preparations were in hand for the monthly barn dance. I was looking forward to it, hoping to meet more of the ranch workers and neighbouring families. On the night it was to take place I took extra care with my appearance, wearing one of my new fashionable dresses, although it did cross my mind that if my dancing partners were all in the image of the driver who had collected me from the halt I need not be so meticulous.

I was pleasantly surprised when I entered the barn. It had been thoroughly cleaned, and beautifully decorated with bunting and greenery. Three fiddlers were sat on hay bales ready to play, and a delicious smell of barbecued beef was wafting through the door. I had earlier made a boiling of sweet corn, and bowls of diced potato salad, and as usual the neighbours had made sure that there was no shortage of fruit pies for afterwards.

Having no acquaintance with the ranch workers or visitors, I felt a little nervous when first entering the barn. I was relieved to see Peggy, a stockman's wife who did the cleaning and laundry up at the house, and Mr Roache, seeing my uncertainty, took my hand and introduced me to as many people as he could. As the music struck up I was besieged by partners all claiming a dance. I didn't flatter myself it was because of my charms, well knowing that a single woman was a rarity on the prairie. There were men of all ages competing to dance, both with me and the other women, and the disappointed made do with a male partner; often a common sight at a prairie barn dance, to see two bearded husky males clutching each other as they pranced around the floor.

Some of the men were cowboys, who often did a winter stint on the big ranches, riding horseback through the winter months to keep check on any wandering cattle, and they usually stayed on until spring to help herd the steers to market, or the nearby railway halt. Mostly younger men, they were huddled together by the door, and seemed apart from the other workers. One in particular I noticed, a tall rangy figure with eyes that scanned the barn with a cool indifference, and although his feet were tapping in time to the music made no move to join the dancers. He was a handsome man, his hair bleached by countless summer suns, and a deep tanned skin that highlighted the blue of his eyes. He must have sensed my scrutiny because he flashed me an arrogant careless look, and then rudely turned away.

I felt a little peeved by his manner, and thought him a mite too full of his own importance, and decided that if he did condescend to ask me to dance I would firmly refuse him. And not lacking partners I put him from my mind, and simply enjoyed the dancing.

Over the next few weeks I occasionally saw the tall cowboy, crossing the yard or riding on his black horse across the paddock behind the house. He would practise his rodeo tricks unaware of a hidden spectator peering through the kitchen window. Peggy said his name was Art and he was a regular seasonal worker at the Roache ranch; not a popular man she confided, his manner too abrupt, and his arrogance disliked.

I was taken by surprise at the next barn dance when he invited me to dance, and contrary to my previous decision I accepted. He really was a very handsome young man, and despite him being at least a decade my junior I did find him attractive. He seemed a man of few words, but his tight grip around my waist, and the closeness of his body made his lack of conversation quite redundant.

Afterwards we sat on a hay bale and ate our supper together. He told me he was born in Arizona of American parents, but had been orphaned whilst young, and had been raised by an uncle who was a stockman on a large ranch. From an early age he had ridden with the cowboys, rounding up cattle and learning the skills that eventually led him to the rodeo circuit. He had been in Canada for ten years and had no inclination to return to America. For someone who was known to be reclusive I found him very talkative. I was more reserved with my history, only telling him I was a widow, and originally from the Old Country.

We fell into the habit of meeting at the barn whenever he and I were free, and I began to look forward to seeing his lanky figure stood across the yard waiting for me to join him. As to be expected it set some tongues wagging, and I believe Art endured a lot of mockery from his fellow workers, some referring I'm sure to the age difference between us. I too had felt concern at my giving him ten years or more, but he shrugged it off and said he had never thought of me as his senior. With his diffidence regarding compliments, I wasn't sure what he actually did think of me.

By Christmas I was nearing the end of my initial three month contract, and although Mrs Roache was making a good recovery she implied that I would be welcome to stay longer. Missing her sister who had returned to her own family I believe she liked the companionship, and was loathe for me to go. And in truth I was happy to stay, content for now to spend the winter in this lovely warm house with amiable people. But another reason I wanted to stay on was my growing attraction to Art.

My emotions were all to pieces, and I was finding it difficult to retain my normal good sense. Realistically I thought us totally unsuited: he was a young cowboy, who drifted from place to place with nowhere to call home, and I was a twice-married older woman who had sons nearer to his age, and who, if I was completely honest was still in love with my late husband Mac. But there was a strong attraction between us, and I was unwilling to let it go.

Together, Mrs Roache and I had served a traditional Christmas dinner to all the cowboys, and to those of the stockyard who were not married or had any family to go to. Mr Roache had been very generous in giving me a large Christmas bonus and an increase in my wage. I felt a little sheepish in accepting it, remembering the goodly sum I had in the Vancouver bank, but I think he saw me as a struggling widow who would be in need of some extra cash. I had never divulged to anyone that I'd had the proceeds from the sale of Mac's farm, which had later financed Pine Valley House, and then that too had yielded a profit.

Art joined us for our festive dinner. In company he retreated to his former unsociable manner, and barely spoke a word, although he did caress my foot under the table with his own, causing me to blush. I had been touched by the small gift he'd given me, a pretty silver pendent which I now wore alongside my precious locket. He had obviously made the effort to ride into Wainwright to buy it, as nothing so fine was to be found in the ranch store.

Our flirtation continued as such over the winter months. We still met up in the shelter of the barn, where he talked of his desire for spring to come, bringing with it the start of the rodeo season. We had never discussed a future together, and I concluded from his urgency to leave the ranch that we didn't have one.

Soon the snow was starting to thaw, and green shoots of grass were showing through the melting ice. The cowboys were already rounding up the steers ready to be branded, and preparing the weaker ones for market. Most of the boys would go on the rodeo trail, but some would look for summer work, driving cattle to more lavish pastures.

The evening before the rodeo group was due to leave I had arranged to meet Art in the barn as usual. I felt confused as to my feelings about him, or about his for me. I accepted that once he'd left our relationship would end, his circuit would take him all over Canada, and even into America if the work was there. He took me completely by surprise by suggesting I go with him; I was unsure on what terms he was thinking of, and said so. He offered marriage if I was willing.

Two days later I followed him to Wainwright where we would arrange to be married. Mr and Mrs Roache were disappointed at my leaving so abruptly, and cautioned me against such a hasty decision. I was sorry to leave them, as they had been very kind to me, but I knew that Mrs Roache was well now, and could manage on her own. And as to their caution, I had enough doubts of my own without taking notice of theirs.

Always having a reckless streak that age had not improved, I abandoned my uncertainties, and plunged into matrimony without any further hesitation.

Wainwright, 9th of April 1923.

Buffalo Park

When Art and I first married we spent a winter living in the Buffalo Park. We lived in lodgings on the Park's boundary, Art working with the other boys who looked after the buffalo herds. I had been offered a job too, assisting with the cooking in the boys lodging house. The buffalo workers were always called the boys despite many of them being middle aged.

Buffalo Park belonged to the Canadian Government, and had been set up to preserve the Buffalo whose numbers had drastically declined; having been hunted to excess in the latter years the herds were rapidly depleting. The park itself consisted of over a thousand acres of prime grassland, the whole protected by a wire fence. The buffalo were allowed to freely roam the land during the summer months, and were brought into more sheltered areas for the winter.

There were over seven thousand of these strange creatures in the park when we lived there. They were fascinating animals, looking so ungainly, and yet could easily outrun a horse. Their fur grew thick and shaggy in the winter, nature's gift to keep out the cold. You could freely walk amongst them with no fear, but how they hated horses, and would give chase at the sight of one. Their fur is like a huge blanket when they shed it in the spring, very soft to touch, and can be spun and made into warm socks or undercoats. Buffalo meat is very tasty too, and undetectable from beef.

Being such a versatile animal they were highly prized by hunters, as one mounted head alone could be worth a hundred dollars. In time I grew quite fond of them, and despite their size found them to be docile and compliant, although I did see one boy badly injured when he'd foolishly tried to take a buffalo calf from the herd and was attacked. They kept in herds, and rather sweet I thought was the practise of surrounding the little ones in winter to keep them warm. The park was also home to a large number of deer and moose.

The park in winter was very cold reaching forty degrees below zero at times. I helped the park manager's wife cook for the twenty men who lived and worked with the buffalo. Their work was hard, having to constantly drag great bales of hay out to the herds, and keeping the animals' drinking water free from ice was a full time occupation. They also oversaw the breeding lines, experimenting with crossing the buffalo with domestic bulls, resulting with their offsprings being known as Cattal. It produced fine animals but they were hybrids.

The boys' appetites were legendry, and I'd never seen such large amounts of food demolished as I witnessed at Buffalo Park. At 5 a.m. they would have porridge, bacon, egg and fried potatoes, followed by pancakes and doughnuts. At noon they came in for dinner, and always the same menu, thick soup, giant steaks with yet more fried potatoes, and usually a boiled pudding and sweet cakes. Come six-o-clock and they trooped back in for more meat, mashed potato with gravy, and cookies and bottled fruit for dessert. And this was all accompanied by fresh baked bread and countless cups of tea. But they were all as lean as Art, and were always complaining of hunger.

I had never worked so hard before, not even at the Station house, and I wondered how Dolly Walker, the manager's wife had managed it all by herself before I'd arrived. She and her husband ran the whole park, he had responsibility for the buffalo herd, and she for the welfare of the boys who worked there. Art and I lived in lodgings outside the wire, but the others lived in dormitory accommodation in close proximity to the buffalos' winter paddocks.

I would travel in each morning with Art in the old truck he had recently purchased. One afternoon I needed to be back in our lodgings before Art had finished work, so I decided to cross the paddock and take a short cut by climbing over the wire fence, which would take me home without the need for transport. It was bitterly cold, but I was well wrapped up, and had thought it a little adventure. I cut through the herd with no problems and reached the boundary fence without mishap, although the biting cold had made my eyes water, and my feet and hands were freezing. I realised on closer inspection that the fence was considerably higher than I'd first thought. Not one to be daunted I decided to take a run and try to clear it in one giant leap.

I was almost successful, but had nor reckoned on there being a thin strand of barbed wire along the top of the fence, and consequently my skirt got tangled up in it, and left me dangling on the wire in a most indelicate manner. I was trapped in this predicament for what seemed a very long time, and it didn't help my peace of mind to have the buffalo come to inspect me. Although happily it was their curiosity that saved me from a likely death due to frostbite, as one of the boys came to see what was attracting the herd to be lingering around the fence. I was not too pleased at his laughter when first sighting me, but was in no position to scold him.

It took me a long time to live that escapade down, and it was only my grim looks that put a stop to the jesting. Art later showed me places in the fence where it could be unhooked to allow a passage through it, but I thought it a little late in the day to enlighten me, particularly as the 'boy' in question had received full sight of my underwear.

With better weather in the spring the buffalo were let free to roam in the parkland, but beforehand had to be branded. It took a week to complete the job, as they were shepherded a few at a time into pens that were called corrals, and then each were branded with a hot branding iron that had been heated to a fiery red before being put sizzling on to the animals rump. The odour of burning hide was most unpleasant, and caused the waiting animals to be skittish, being none too happy to start with, and sensing that their turn was yet to come. The boys had to watch out for lethal kicks from the usually docile animals, and most had bruises to show when the branding finished. But once let free the animals quickly got over it and forgave their keepers, going off happily to eat the fresh new shoots of grass in the park.

We had a good winter on the buffalo farm, and I was a little sad to leave, but it was rodeo time and Art was keen to get away. Mrs Walker did ask if I would stay on, as she and I had become good friends, and she really did need the help. But being newly married I felt my place was with Art, and I was interested to see him perform his rodeo skills.

I really missed the park, and its buffalos after we left, but it always makes me smile when I think of them and remember my undignified tussle with the wire fence, and often wonder what the inquisitive animals must have thought of the strange creature suspended atop of it with an expanse of pink bloomers on show.

The Horseshoe Inn, Calgary. 2nd of June 1924.

The War Memorial

It was a long time since I had been to Edmonton, and I was surprised by its growth. It had expanded into quite a city, the wooden built shops and walkways were now made of brick, and the roads paved with wide side walks. Hotels had sprung up on land which on my previous visit had just been empty vacant plots.

The town unlike Vancouver was bitter cold in winter, and even in the summer had a chill about it. I remember Mac telling me that it had originated as a fort, built for the Hudson's Bay Company, its wooden stockade protecting the major fur trade of the area. Despite it being on the edge of a wilderness it had always attracted settlers and trappers to its hostile terrain. He had visited the area many times as a child with his father, living for months out in the wilds whilst trapping furs.

I had accompanied Art who was to do a rodeo. We had taken a room in a small mean lodging house in an old part of the town, which still had a look of its former frontier settlement about it, its humble wooden shacks dispersed between more refined buildings. Our room was none too clean, and whilst Art went to find his fellow cowboys I gave it a thorough scrub down, and was not happy with the bed linen either, the rough calico sheets were grimy and torn. I was beginning to find this constant moving from one shabby lodgings to another very wearing, and I had not thought when first marrying Art how distasteful I would find it.

The last time I was here was when Mac and I stayed overnight on our way to our new lives on the farm. I had felt some reluctance to return, as there were too many memories of him to make my visit comfortable. But I had committed myself to following the summer rodeos with Art, and had no longer a home to call my own.

One thing I had determined to do whilst here, was to visit the new war memorial that had been recently erected to honour the fallen in the Great War. I had inquired of the landlady as to its whereabouts, and she had directed me to a small plot of land that had been donated by the town, to give tribute to the memory of its people who had fought in France with the local regiment, and who had not returned. I wanted to see it to pay my own homage to Mac and his fellow men, who had lost their lives in such a wasteful foolish war.

As I neared the memorial I could see the powerful statue on its plinth, a black marble soldier weighed down with his equipment and rifle, gazing out with empty eyes towards the horizon. I looked into his face, and thought of all the mothers, widows and children left without their loved ones, and of the barren farms denied the strong arms behind a plough.

There were flowers and small mementos laid at the feet of the statue. I had come empty handed, but took a comb out of my hair, kissed it in memory of Mac and placed it alongside the other contributions. Walking around the plinth to gain another view I noticed a brass plate fastened to its side, and saw the row of names that were engraved on it. With excitement I searched for Mac's, but could find no sign of it, and after anxiously searching from top to bottom came to realise that his name was not inscribed. I was disturbed by its absence, I recognised other names: John Wilson, the son of old neighbours, who had enlisted the same day as Mac, Percy Laidlow who had travelled alongside him when they had joined the regiment.

I thought there must be some mistake, the engraver had made an error, or the paperwork sent from the war front had accidentally missed out a name. I searched again, perhaps I had overlooked it, or the spelling was wrong, but no it wasn't there. I felt a chill come over me as an unbidden thought crossed my mind. Had Mac's name been omitted because of his Cree blood, surely not, whatever his birth his blood had stained the earth, the same as all the other soldiers who had been given the dignity of recognition. I vowed as I stood looking up at the statue, that Mac's name would be put there whatever I had to do to ensure it.

I was agitated when I returned to the lodging house, and sat awhile trying to determine the best way to set about rectifying the grave affront to my beloved Mac's memory. When Art returned I told him of my dismay that my second husband's name had not been included on the memorial. He thought I was over reacting, and taking no heed of my distress he continued to wash and dress, preparing for that afternoon's show.

I too dressed in my smartest suit, and as I placed my best hat firmly on my head I was resolute that I was not leaving the town until I'd had some answers. My first call was at the local attorney's office, hoping to get advice on who was responsible for the wording on the memorial. Unknowingly I had gone to the right person, as well as being a man of law he was the head of the local councillors who had been responsible for the fund raising, and dedication of the memorial.

He seemed genuinely upset by the oversight they had made in omitting Mac's name, and said the list of names had been compiled by the War Office. There had been some mistakes made, as one name submitted turned out to be a farmer's son who was in fact very much alive, having returned from the war unscathed.

Although sympathetic to my distress he said there was little he could do about the oversight, as the brass plaque was complete with no way now of adding my late husband's name. I started to feel anger rising at his casual dismissal of Mac's memory, and asked him where he himself had spent the war years, not in the midst of battle I presumed. He blushed, and said that was quite beside the point, and if I didn't mind he would like me to leave his office as he was a busy man.

I'd found myself ushered out into the street and his door firmly closed. I was seething, and had to take deep breaths before continuing on my way. As I stood on the sidewalk I noticed a news vendor selling the daily Edmonton paper and was immediately taken with an idea. I made my way to the newspaper offices and asked to see the editor. Within minutes I was sitting in his office, a cup of tea in my hand, and an attentive ear listening to my story. Mr Muldoon was the newspaper's proprietor as well as its editor, feature writer and chief tea maker. He was a squat cheerful little man who had come out from Ireland as a young reporter, and who through his hard work had risen to own his own newspaper. I had liked and trusted him on sight, and had felt his empathy as I told him the tale, he'd offered me a grubby handkerchief when I burst into tears, and such was my distress I used it.

He said he'd lost a brother in the war, and could well understand my desire to have Mac's name on the memorial. "And dammed if we don't get it put on," he said, and then apologised in his broad Irish accent for his swearing. I already felt much better, and was sure he would find a way to achieve it.

The following day the newspaper's headlines proclaimed a miscarriage of justice, with a picture of the war memorial on its front page. The leading story was of a hero who had sacrificed his life in Canada's name, and who was not being honoured by the townspeople who had sent him to war. On the second page was a picture of me, and my plea for my late husband's name to be inscribed alongside the others of his regiment.

I was amazed at the power of the press, within hours of the newspaper's issue the councillor's office was besieged by people demanding that Mac's name be added to the memorial. The newspaper was inundated with offers of hospitality on my behalf, and the soldier's statue was surrounded by flowers, and pieces of paper were stuck to it with Mac's name printed on.

I was touched by the people who came up to me in the street and clasped my hands, offering their support, and even money to help get his name put in its rightful place. The councillors, mindful of coming elections visited me to say they had decided to add a small brass plate to the memorial, and have Mac's name inscribed on it.

Before leaving Edmonton I was able to attend the ceremony to unveil it. The townspeople cheered as the small plaque appeared, and Mr Muldoon once more gave me his grubby handkerchief as I wept tears of pride. I was satisfied that justice had been done, and my loved one's name was where it should have been, alongside his fallen comrades.

I went back once more before departing, and gently traced my fingers across the lettering, whispering to myself, "Rest in peace, James Alistair Mc Kenzie – my darling Mac."

Edmonton. 20th of July 1924.

The Cowboy

I'd married Art Dunning early summer in a small Wainwright Methodist chapel – the first of my three marriages to be solemnized in an actual consecrated building.

I had been unsure of it happening right up to the moment I took my vows, beset by doubts, none of which I'd had in my two previous marriages. I had loved William with a young girl's innocent intensity, and had entered into our marriage with every intent of its continuing happiness. I was older and wiser when I married Mac, but secure in the knowledge that I had found my soul mate, and had never doubted his steadfastness.

In truth I think I had been flattered by Art's courtship, and earlier somewhat piqued by his studied indifference. To be admired by a handsome virile man, who was many years younger than yourself, was very gratifying. But some inner instinct warned me of taking up his offer of marriage, not least the fact that I had been my own counsel for many years, and might not take kindly to having a man dictate my life. Offsetting this fear was my loneliness, and the need to have a loving arm to lean on. I visualised my old age without such a prop, and felt some anxiety as to my future.

Initially, despite my concerns we'd rubbed along very well together, he was ardent and at first keen to please me. We followed the rodeos during the summer months and led a nomadic lifestyle, bedding down where we could, often sleeping in the truck. That first winter of our marriage had been happily spent at the buffalo farm, but the following year we took casual lodgings, where I had stayed alone whilst he worked the cattle trails. This had been a very lonely time for me, living in a strange environment, and feeling unhappy with the impermanence of my existence.

I'd become depressed and unlike myself, and my sister wrote to say that I was probably undergoing the change of life, but when Art joined me in the spring he showed quite plainly his distaste for my fretful moods. Until the rodeo circuit started he was no longer earning a wage, and insisted I find the money for our living costs. He was often aggressive, raising his voice, and on one occasion his hand: this last I found hard to forgive, and our relationship deteriorated even more.

Three years married and bitterly regretting it. My pride, which was always my downfall wouldn't allow me to admit it to anyone, and we continued our life as before except that I decided to no longer follow the rodeo shows with him, and took permanent lodgings in Vancouver. I could have purchased a property, I had enough funds in the bank, but this fortunately I'd always kept secret from Art, knowing he would have demanded every penny of it. Feeling more settled I had taken a job as housekeeper at a large new hotel by the waterfront, and this combined with my husband's lengthy absences had lifted my spirits.

But he had finished doing the cattle trails, preferring to spend the winter months living off my earnings in Vancouver's milder climate. Tales came back to me of his womanising in the summer on the rodeo circuit, and of his liaisons closer to home, but in truth I no longer cared.

To all appearances we seemed a happy couple, but this was far from the truth. I had on occasion gone into work with bruising on my cheek, and excused this by blaming my own clumsiness. I well knew that if I had been of a more placid nature he might not have resorted to brutality, but I had always had an inner spirit in me, and wouldn't allow myself to cower against his violence, despite my vulnerability.

In my darkest moments I thought of Mac, and his gentle loving ways, and felt the old bitterness rise in me that he had been so cruelly taken. He was always in my dreams, and what torture it was to wake and find him gone.

Such was my unhappiness I had fantasies of killing Art, and often after a bitter row I would take comfort from devising a painful death for him. But despite my hatred, I didn't have the courage. The only things that kept me sane were his regular departure for the rodeos, and my writing in this journal.

I often wondered if I should discard the many journals I had kept, not wanting Art to read and mock them. But I knew I never would, it would be like destroying my very existence, and I couldn't bear to lose the reassurance, and identity that they gave me.

Blake's Lodging House, Vancouver. 12th of May 1926.

The Lake

From the first moment I set eyes on Lake Solitude, I knew it was the place where I wanted to be for the rest of my life. The overwhelming beauty of its location stunned me. It was like finding paradise when least expecting it.

Its clear blue waters reflected the fringe of the tall pine trees that surrounded it, and seemed untouched by any hand, other than its creator. Canada had some spectacular scenery, but none to my mind that surpassed this.

It was quite by chance that I had discovered it. Picking up a small leaflet in the store I had seen notice of a land auction to be held in Vancouver the following week. Unknown to Art I had been thinking for a while to purchase some land. Despite his probing I had never divulged the amount of money that I had salted away in a Vancouver bank, placing it there after leaving Black Ridge Gap. He knew I had a regular income, but from where it came I had not disclosed.

I think he'd thought it a monthly allowance from my family in England, and I confess that I had let him persist in that belief. Some sixth sense had prevented me from divulging it at the beginning of our relationship – a fortunate decision, as I came to realise quite early in my marriage.

With Art working the rodeo circuit I was free to make my own amusement, and the auction catalogue had whetted my appetite to own land again. The agent offered to drive me to view some of the advertised plots, the first one being the lake and its surrounding acreage.

I had no desire to see any other, despite the agent advising it. Lake Solitude was all that I could ever hope for. It was aptly named, set well back from the winding coastal road, and only found by following a narrow trail inland. Its seclusion appealed to me, my natural tendency to solitude had been well honed by prairie life.

The agent agreed to place my bid, it not being expected in Vancouver's rigid social codes that a woman would attend an auction, let alone make her own bid. I'd felt annoyed by this restriction which I considered more in keeping with the old country, but such was my longing for this land I was willing to keep my views to myself.

My bid was successful, and what joy I felt, the lake was mine. Whilst dealing with the solicitors I'd made a new will, bequeathing all my property to my two sons, and making them my executors. If I died before Art, not a penny of Mac's money would he get.

I kept my purchase secret, visiting the lake whenever I craved some peace, or simply to take delight in its ownership. I had made enquiries about building a house overlooking its placid waters, and was already drawing up plans for a simple building which would have a large timber deck that reached out over the water's edge.

My secret made me happy, and I would daydream, imagining Mac and I living there. I know he would have loved it as much as I did. And as I planned the house it was always with Mac in mind, I would talk to him and ask his advice.

Sadly it was a foolish dream. Art returned from the rodeos at the end of the season, and soon discovered where I was disappearing to. When realising what I'd done he raged, and later that night ill-treated me. He had always been a bully, and quite early in the marriage I had become a victim of his ill temper.

He warned me that I would never get away from him, he told me daily that I was old and ugly, and should think myself lucky he'd married me. I had learnt to hold my tongue; in the past I would have retaliated, only to have his fist in my face.

He went off in his truck to look at my lake, or as he called it, his property.

It gave me a secret pleasure to think of his rage if he knew of the legitimate will that was placed in the safety of a Vancouver bank. Amazingly he approved of my purchase, calling it a tidy little property that could only rise in value.

I had the timber house built to my planned design, and moved in the following spring. Art was away again, doing another circuit of the rodeo shows and would not be back until fall. I was happy to be there on my own, and revelled in the peace and quiet of my new home. Each evening as night fell I would walk to the water's edge, look up at the stars and converse with Mac. I felt very close to him, and knew he was watching over me. Without that knowledge my life would have been worthless.

Within a few months everything changed, and my new found peace ended. Art had been transported home in the back of his truck, both legs broken after a bad fall whilst working at the Calgary Stampede. He didn't take kindly to being housebound, and nor did I at his enforced stay at home. But worse was to follow, his legs failed to heal, and he was left with a permanent severe limp.

It was the end of his rodeo career, and he became depressed and very hard to live with. I decided to use the remainder of my money to buy him a bigger truck, so that he could carry haulage for a living. He was somewhat surprised by my generosity, but really it was for my own benefit as I desperately needed him from under my feet.

With the summer months approaching I'd had an idea to make some extra money to replenish my savings. I had a spare bedroom, which I advertised in the Vancouver papers, offering good clean holiday accommodation in peaceful surroundings; with the added bonus of private fishing.

Weary city dwellers deluged me with letters wanting to reserve the room. I could have rented it many times over, such was the demand. After a few summers I had saved enough to have two small cabins erected across the lake, well out of sight of my nightly conversations with Mac.

Such was their success I invested in another two, and within five years I had a thriving business. Totally unexpected, but very satisfying, as I had a pride in my achievement, and also a regular income. And of course the added bonus of still being able to enjoy the peace and tranquillity of my lake for six months of the year.

As I often told Mac, I was as content here as I could be anywhere without him by my side.

Lake Solitude. 12th of September 1931.

An Unexpected Reunion

The frenzied barking of the yard dogs had roused me abruptly from a brief afternoon nap. I hastily smoothed my hair and straightened my apron before taking a quick glance out of the window. I saw the shadow of a man across the porch steps, but the strong sunshine blinded me to his identity. It had to be a stranger to have caused the dogs to make such a rumpus, I was not expecting any callers, and Art wouldn't be back before nightfall, and even if he had returned early the dogs knew better than to provoke his anger by their din.

I hesitated before opening the unlocked door, but knowing that the fly screen was bolted on the inside I felt safe enough to open the inner one, and cautiously pulled it back to view the stranger who was standing there.

I saw a tall, well-built young man leaning against the porch rail; he was clean shaven and smartly dressed, with a somewhat familiar look about him. Feeling reassured I asked him his business, and why he was calling on us in such an out of the way spot. He didn't reply, but looked searchingly at my face.

I too was scrutinizing him, noting the strong set of his jaw, and the contour of his head, the thick dark curly hair. My heart missed a beat, I didn't need an introduction, I knew who the stranger was – I unbolted the fly screen, putting a trembling hand on the door frame to steady myself.

"Eddie, or is it Thomas?" I whispered. "I can't believe it's you."

I must have looked about to faint because a strong young arm supported me, and gently sat me down on the porch steps. "I'm Thomas, Mama," he said.

He sat down next to me and took my hands in his; we were both crying and talking at the same time. His voice alone evoked so many memories, the soft Derbyshire accent, the mischievous look in his eyes, so like his father's – I was shaken to my very being, it was as if William had returned from the grave.

We sat there holding hands, hugging, crying and laughing, and all the while the dogs were snarling and trying to loosen their chains. I took him inside the cabin, and found myself too shaken to lift the coffee pot from the stove. He found the cups and poured for both of us. I could only stare in wonder at this fine young man, one of my precious sons, who by some miracle had appeared on my doorstep.

He had still been in short pants the last time I'd seen him, a small figure standing on the quayside in Liverpool, bravely waving goodbye to his mother aboard the big ship taking her to Canada. I remember looking at his little figure, growing smaller as the ship moved away from the dock, my eyes blinded by tears, but just recognising him and his brother, dressed in the blue and white sailor suits that they had worn that day, and the jaunty little caps that they were both waving. Over the years, and despite the portraits that my brother had sent, that was always the picture that had remained in my head.

All the time I had been in Canada my dream and fervent hope had been that my beloved sons would join me, and share my life again, but it never happened. My brother had kept them on the family farm, and cherished them as his own.

We talked until night approached and I heard Art's lorry rattling on the track. I busied myself preparing a meal, my voice quite hoarse with so much unaccustomed talk and emotion. My thoughts were still in the past and my mind adjusting to all that Thomas had told me – he had some family pictures to show me and I marvelled at the portrait of my eldest son Edward, and his wife, and young family. To see Edward now a respected farmer, and so much like my own dear father. And Rebecca his wife, the village school mistress that he'd courted and married five years gone, and the two dear little children – my grandchildren. I was shocked at my brother's likeness, I no longer recognised him as such, a picture of an elderly man with the pain of his ailments etched harshly on his face, and his wife, my sister-in-law with the same remembered sour look on hers. But I was being uncharitable, and quick to scorn because both of them had reared my boys with unquestionable love and devotion. And looking at my grown Thomas sat here in my kitchen I had no quarrel with their parenting.

I heard Art's footsteps outside, and the groan of the porch chair as he sat to take off his boots. My happiness subsided. I felt the immediate knot of fear in my stomach that his arrival always brought. I could see by the expression on his face that he was angered by the stabling of a stranger's horse. I hastily introduced my son to his scowling step-father. Talking too fast, and somewhat anxiously, as I told of my joy at his finding us and how clever he was to have tracked us down in such an isolated place. They shook hands, and I was proud to see my son's civility and good manners, but was deeply ashamed by Art's surly response, his only retort being to ask how long Thomas intended to stay. Stung to anger I replied for him, "For as long as he would like to," and in my heart I hoped for ever.

Long after Art had taken to his bed Thomas and I sat out on the porch. It was a warm summer's night and we talked until daybreak, watching the sun rise in the sky, marvelling together at its beauty. So many times I had sat like this, spellbound by the wonder of the scene and thinking if only I could share it with my sons, and now at last I was able to, at least with one of them.

Thomas had quickly realised that my marriage was not a happy one, and expressed his concern for me. He intended to travel to Vancouver where he had been offered employment as a butcher, a trade he had been apprenticed to back in England. He hoped to settle in the city and make a home, and bring out his sweetheart whom he'd left back in Derbyshire. He told me that there would be a home there for me too if I needed it, but whilst enjoying the warm feeling that his offer gave me, I joked and said perhaps his future wife might have something to say about that. I was simply happy to know that he was in the same province as I, and would be near enough to occasionally visit.

After an early breakfast Thomas said it was time to leave, Art having made it clear the night before that he wouldn't be a welcome guest. I was unhappy with this decision, but he said he didn't want to cause any discord, and had to return the horse to the livery stable that he'd hired it from before catching his train back to Vancouver. We tightly hugged, and promised to keep in close contact now that we had found each other again. I watched him ride down the track, waving until I no longer had sight of him, and staying at the gate until my agitation and his dust trail had settled, and then reluctantly going back indoors, already suffering from his absence.

How I would have loved to have been riding alongside him, not wanting to lose his physical presence after so many years without sight of him. But I accepted that he needed to make his own way in the world, and what finer place could he have chosen to do it in? I hoped that he would grow to love this beautiful country as much as I did. I walked back into the cabin, back to my surly husband and the hostile marriage that we shared. I had made a mistake in marrying Art and had to live with the fact that he had wed me for my money; my only satisfaction came from the knowledge that I owned this lake and the cabins, and no bullying disgruntled husband would ever prise it off me.

Lake Solitude. 17th of June 1932.

175

Taking Tea at Lake Solitude

It was quite by chance that I found I had an unexpected talent. Two of my regular guests were a couple by the name of Wilton who came up to the lake most weekends in the summer, having a permanent booking of one of the cabins. I'd grown quite friendly with Eunice, Henry Wilton's wife. She would come to the house whilst he was fishing and we would share a pot of tea. They were a nice congenial pair who loved Lake Solitude as much as I did. They seemed very happy together, and sometimes I would envy their easy relationship. The only sadness they shared was their lack of children, married for eight years and no sign of motherhood for Eunice, and this was obviously a great disappointment to them both.

I was telling her one day of my grandmother's gift of being able to see into the future, and of my own occasional glimpses of things to come. She asked if I could read the tea leaves left in her cup, and laughing I said I would try. Half in jest I studied her cup, and strangely the leaves took shape and I saw quite clearly the outline of two identical babies. I looked up, and without thought told her she would have twins before the year was out. I had unwittingly upset her, she believed I was mocking her childless state and she abruptly left the house.

It caused embarrassment between us, and afterwards she rarely came to see me. The following summer they booked again, and I was out front when they arrived, and was dumbfounded to see Henry unload a large pram from the back of their station wagon. My astonishment grew when Eunice pushed it over to the house a while later, and introduced me to the two bonnie little girls that it carried.

Their happiness at being parents was obvious, although it had come about through tragedy. Henry's sister had died in childbirth, leaving the twins motherless, and their father unable to cope. So Henry and Eunice had taken them, and were in the process of adoption. My tea leaf reading had come true, they had become the proud parents of identical twins exactly a year to the day I had prophesised.

Art ridiculed my gift, saying it had simply been a lucky guess. I would have dearly liked to have read his, but I noticed he always rinsed out his cup before I had chance to see the leaves. I believed he was afraid of what I might see, or of what I might tell him I'd seen, and I admit I possibly would have embroidered the truth a little to alarm him.

News had spread about the readings, and sometimes I regretted my success as people would drive to the lake to ask me to read for them. Often a car load of women would turn up at the door taking no notice of my reluctance to open it, and would set up a spirit stove to make tea in the front yard.

The only time I had felt fear at one of these sessions was as I read a young woman's empty cup, even as I took it from her hand I felt a chill down my spine, and was reluctant to look inside. I could only see violence, and a black menacing end for the pretty girl who was smiling as she awaited my findings. I told her that I was feeling tired and could see nothing in her leaves, she left disappointed, her friends giggling and saying she had wanted to know if her boyfriend would propose. This was the dark side of my new found talent, and one that dismayed me.

I had come to realise that I'd always had this ability, but had never before utilised it. On recollection there were numerous times when I had clearly seen events either about to happen or already occurred. I had known before receiving news of my father's death that he had gone, having had a vision of him lying in the top field clutching his heart. And of course with Mac's death I'd felt the sharp stab of pain as the German bullet found its mark. I had never before admitted to myself that I had my grandmother's gift, but I had to recognise it now and deal with the disquiet it gave me. Through use my visions had become clearer, and now when I took my usual evening walk to the lakeside I not only communicated with Mac I also had sight of his spectral shape. These brief encounters filled me with joy.

Art told people I was deranged, talking to myself, and coming back to the house with a radiant look on my face. His disparagement and the local gossip didn't worry me, I had proof that Mac was watching over me, and was patiently waiting for us to be reunited again. And that was enough to keep me sane.

Lake Solitude. 27th of August 1933.

All God's Creatures

I have never been afraid of animals, unlike my sister Lucy, who was terrified of dogs, having been bitten by a family pet when small. Despite my lack of fear I did have respect for the danger they could offer, well remembering my father having two cracked ribs from a fractious cow, and once I saw a farm hand tossed by an over-excited bull as he led it to a mate.

When first arriving in Canada I had been dubious about its wildlife. I'd read about grizzly bears attacking people, and had heard tales of packs of hungry wolves roaming the countryside. Before leaving home my brothers had teased me about the wild creatures who would be wanting to make a meal of me. I had laughed off their remarks, but they had sowed a seed of disquiet that had seriously alarmed me when, after reaching Blue River Halt, I'd found myself quite alone, and surrounded by total isolation. The hours spent waiting for William caused my imagination to run riot, and until he came had thought myself liable to harm from any passing bear or hungry wolf.

He had laughed when I'd told him of my fears, and said he had only seen one bear since arriving in Canada, and that had been a fair distance away. I personally thought that was one bear too many, but had felt some reassurance that the prairies were not rife with them. It was in fact the howling of a wolf pack that had helped William and I to ease the awkwardness of our first night together, with me yelling for him to come back inside the cabin when I'd heard their blood curdling cries. Not realising that sound carries long distances on the open prairie, my fear of William being torn apart by a hungry canine mob was quite groundless.

Thankfully Canadian wildlife was just as timid of humans as I was of them, and unless provoked, generally minded their own business. I had occasionally seen a prairie fox slinking its way across the farmyard, and would bang a pan against the cabin door to frighten him off, as he was usually after one of my laying hens. The coyote was our biggest pest; these were small prairie wolves who were fearless, and who would attack a horse if hungry. William always carried his rifle when venturing out, and would aim to kill the leader of the pack, which would scare the followers away. The noise they made was quite unnerving, and even when safe inside the cabin I would feel a chill down my spine.

The first time I saw a bear close up was many years later in Black Ridge Gap. Despite the timbered forests being their natural habitat I'd had no sightings of any, and having been told by Billie that the noise of the saw mill kept them away, I had felt quite safe walking the forest paths around Pine Valley House and the logging camp. My bear encounter happened one winter evening when I'd slipped down to the camp to have a quick word with Martha. It was dark, but a bright moon lit up the familiar path. Normally I would be accompanied back by one of my lodgers, but wanting to get home I didn't wait for an escort, not liking to interrupt their leisure time.

Almost in sight of the house I heard the breaking of twigs on the path behind me, and swung round, expecting to see one of my lodgers who had followed me home. But it was not a human who was following my tracks, I froze and stood still, it was as if my body had suddenly turned to stone. I was terrified to see within a few feet of me a brown bear. My mind simply stopped functioning, and I stared with vacant eyes at the creature who was following in my footsteps. The bear seemed equally at a loss, and raised himself up on his hind legs and stared back at me, his tiny dark eyes glinting in the moonlight.

I had been told many times the rules of meeting a bear face to face – not to turn and run, but to stand perfectly still and hold your breathing in for as long as you could, playing dead. I had always joked at this advice and said that if I ever met a bear face to face I would be dead, having died instantly of a heart attack.

Now the unthinkable had happened, and I was locked in meditation with a brown bear. In all, the encounter probably only lasted for a few seconds, but it seemed a lifetime, as with a total disregard of the rules of bear etiquette I turned and fled. I ran as I had never ran before, terror giving my feet wings. I thought I could hear the pounding of him behind me, but when I'd reached the safety of the yard I could see no sign of him following me. Once inside the house with the door firmly fastened and legs that had turned to jelly I clung to the staircase for support. When I was calmer I opened up the medicine cabinet and took a tot of my medicinal whiskey.

When my lodgers came in they were surprised to find me with a glass in my hand and the bottle at my side. They were concerned for me, realising what a fright I'd had. Billie said the bear would have come down from the mountain top in search of food, and contrary to popular thought all bears didn't hibernate in winter. They would search rubbish tips hoping to find something edible. Once the snow fell they were restricted in their hunting, and were known to go further, even into urban areas in search of substance, and he said that I had been lucky that the bear had not given chase. All of my lodgers insisted that in future I would be escorted wherever I went, even if it meant curtailing their drinking time, as they always had a rifle handy. I assured them that after the fright I'd had my nocturnal trips would end. I did eventually regain my courage, and started to use the camp tracks again, but always armed with a saucepan and wooden spoon hoping to frighten away any unsuspecting bear with the noise I would make.

Along with other advice I'd been told to make a noise when walking alone as bears didn't like being surprised, and would disappear into the forest at the slightest sound. Not wanting to be surprised either, I would bang my saucepan and loudly sing as I walked the tracks, feeling somewhat foolish, but finding my embarrassment the lesser of the evils. Martha said that she always put the coffee on when she heard the banging echoing through the trees, and my quavering voice reciting poetry or singing God Save The Queen.

Over the years I did see other bears but none so close up as that one. Since moving here to Lake Solitude I often hear bears scrabbling in the trash cans during the night, but they are rarely to be seen in daylight, the dogs usually frightening them away.

My biggest enemy has always been the mosquitoes. We have an unequal aversion to each other, and between July and August I need to completely cover up my skin or they try to eat me alive. It is most uncomfortable in the intense heat of summer to wear stockings and long sleeved shirts, and to be constantly swatting my face. Horse flies are another menace, great ugly insects that fight to land on any bare skin or unprotected food. These nuisances, and the very occasional sightings of bears and wolves, are the only drawback to living in Canada. Sometimes I long for the English countryside with no wild animals waiting to ambush you, and the chance to walk the country lanes without being attacked by poisonous insects. Despite these drawbacks I still have loved my life in this wonderful country, and have come to accept living alongside its natural habitat, and to no longer be intimidated at the howling of a pack of wolves as they traverse the prairie.

Lake Solitude. 16th of September 1933.

Uninvited Guests

Most of the cabins were let out to regular guests, many of whom became good friends. My cabins were known for being clean and tidy, and to tired businessmen and their families from the city, they were a haven of peace and quiet where they could relax, fish a little, or just enjoy the beautiful surroundings of the lake.

Some were taken on a long rental for the whole of the summer months, and I was asked many times if I would sell one, but always declined, as I valued my ownership, and the undisturbed tranquillity that came from my sole occupancy in the winter.

I always had plenty of company during the letting season, the visiting children soon got to know where my cookie tin was kept, and when I was having a baking day their inbuilt sense of smell would lead them to my kitchen door. Their mothers too would head for the deck, filling in the time whilst their husbands were off hunting or fishing, and we would all enjoy drinking coffee and putting the world to right.

The older children would spend their days swimming in the clear waters of the lake or sunbathing on its sandy shore. Occasionally one of them would yell that somebody was out of their depth, and the strongest swimmers amongst them would rouse themselves to swim out to rescue the panicking ones. It was an idyllic summer holiday for the youngsters, who were generally polite and well-behaved. In the evenings they would hold cookouts at the lakeside, grilling the fish or game that their fathers had snared.

Art would be away for most of the holiday season. He still followed the rodeo trail, but now as an onlooker rather than a participant. His once lithe frame was running to fat, and he drank far too much to be safely astride a horse. I gave him enough money for his lodgings, and to frequent the bar where he liked to meet his cronies to boast of his own past skills on the circuit. This arrangement suited us both, as the less we saw of each other the more the marriage was agreeable.

A local lad helped me keep the land tidy, cutting the grass around the cabins, and doing any odd jobs that were too arduous for me to handle. And when summer ended he would assist me in closing up the cabins, boarding the windows and securing the doors. He also filled my wood pile ready for the onslaught of winter. Despite the milder weather that British Columbia enjoyed we still had our share of snow, and the log pile would be close to depletion before spring set in.

I enjoyed the brief time I had after closing my cabins, and before Art returned to give me hassle. I felt more free to communicate with Mac, which I still did every night, but now had peace and quiet to revere our precious time together. It was as I stood by the lakeside waiting for him to join me that I thought I saw a flickering light amongst the trees, but it disappeared and I put it down to my imagination, and as of late my weaker eyesight.

But next morning I was puzzled to find no eggs when I searched the poultry shed, my hens until now being regular layers. And the following day not only was there no eggs, I was also a hen short. I'd heard some squawking in the night, but had thought it a young bear or fox trying its luck, and knowing that my hens were well fastened in I had turned over and gone back to sleep.

After two more days of eggs disappearing, a small churn of milk that had been left out for me on the track vanished too. I began to suspect that I had an uninvited guest, but could see no trace of anyone, and for the first time felt some concern for my safety. I started to carry Art's rifle with me wherever I went, and kept it fully loaded by my bedside at night. I was surprised the dogs had not barked, usually the first to inform me of an intruder. I felt uneasy, but also determined to find my thief.

The next night I followed my normal routine of talking to Mac, and then as usual after supper turned down the lamp as if going to bed. Instead I got warmly dressed and climbed out of the back window to sneak into the trees behind the hen house. I hid for what seemed an hour or more, and was almost about to turn and go back to my bed when I saw a flickering light appear from the back of the furthest cabin. Holding the rifle steady I crouched down, watching the progress of the light as it slowly came towards me.

At last it neared the shed, and I understood the reason why the dogs were not barking: whoever my intruder was, he had a way with animals, as the dogs were virtually slobbering all over him. My eyes had become accustomed to the darkness, and I was able to make out the shape of the figure holding the flickering lamp. He was tall but of a slight build, having the frame of young person, and then as he held the lamp higher I almost gave away my presence, gasping with surprise at the sight of a smaller second figure standing close behind him. It seemed I had two intruders, not just the one that I had expected to find.

I stood silently in the cover of the pines, and watched the taller of the two unlatch the door, whilst the other crept inside to collect my eggs. They were obviously taken by surprise at finding none, and the taller thief joined the other one to share in the search. It was a futile one, because earlier as darkness had fallen, I too had crept in, and taken them all.

Whilst they were occupied in their search I rushed forward and quickly slammed the door shut, putting the bar across to prevent their escape. I expected to hear cursing or a banging at the door, but not a sound came from them, and other than the fluttering of the disturbed birds there was a complete silence. This response baffled me, I had been afraid of violence and was at a loss now to know what to do, as I couldn't keep them prisoner until someone came by to visit me, it could be a week or more.

After a long silence I started to feel concerned: perhaps the shock of their discovery and the fetid stuffiness of the hen house had caused them to suffer asphyxia. I tapped on the door and asked if they were alright, but warned I had a gun which I wasn't frightened to use. Still no reply, and as I debated the wisdom of unbarring the door to check on their welfare, a soft voice said, "Don't shoot, Mrs Dunning, it's me. Amelia, you know me. I'm Amelia Martin."

I put down the gun and breathed a sigh of relief; so one of my intruders was Amelia, the daughter of the Martins, who were regular summer visitors, and not eight weeks ago she had sat on my deck eating homemade cookies. I asked her who was with her, and she said it was Richard Harvey, whom I also knew, he too being a regular visitor with his sister and parents. I quickly unbarred the door and let my two thieves out into the fresh air.

They looked very sheepishly at me, and neither was smelling too good. I told them both to follow me back to the house, and said I hoped that they had a good explanation for their being here. Once in the house I sat them down and waited for them to account for their behaviour. Between the two of them I eventually got the full story – they had run away from home after their parents had forbidden them to meet. A summer romance had developed at the lakeside, and had gained in strength once they were back home, potent enough, despite their youth, to want to marry. Both sets of parents had been totally against the idea, and I did have some sympathy for their concern, with Amelia due to start a teacher's training course that month, and Richard serving the first year of his indenture with a firm of Vancouver solicitors. Despite this awareness I also had some compassion for the young lovers, my own youthful follies not yet forgotten.

Having decided to flee together they had been unsure of a destination, and being somewhat short of money they were limited in the scope of their travel. Having happy memories of Lake Solitude they had decided to make their way here, and had been lucky begging lifts to make it within the day. Richard had removed the bars from a cabin window and they had been hiding there for the last four days, but the food they had with them had soon gone, and consequently they had turned to petty crime.

I surveyed my two criminals and felt sad for them, and for the heartbreak that was surely coming. The pangs of young love burn deep, but I knew that I was going to have to persuade them to go back home. Although I was getting the impression that they were both tired of living rough and being cold and hungry, and would not take much persuasion. After I had cooked them a hot meal, I suggested they bed down in the sitting room for the rest of the night, advising it would be better to make plans when we'd all had some sleep.

Thankfully the next morning they both agreed that they would return home, and I said I would try and arrange a lift for them with the travelling dry goods man who daily delivered in the area. If ever I needed groceries I would walk up the winding track and leave my basket at the entrance, and he would then drive down to take my order. Richard offered to run up and place the basket for me, and sure enough within the hour the van was at the door, the driver surprised at seeing my basket having only called a week ago. In the summer he called daily, always doing a good trade with my guests. He agreed to pick up the young people on his return journey, and take them back to Vancouver. With a few hours to spare I was careful to give them some time together, having an understanding of the pangs of parting from a loved one.

The delivery man came back for them as promised. I kissed them both goodbye and told them to talk things over with their parents, promising that they would not do anything rash, and then maybe things might not seem so desperate. As they drove away I knew that there would be two very relieved families that night, and really hoped that harmony would be restored, and that they would be allowed to see each other.

Neither family ever returned to the lake again, so I will never know the outcome. I like to think that all ended happily.

Lake Solitude, 4th of October 1933.

A Sentence of Death

I knew I was dying, long before the city doctor had diagnosed the growth in my breast. My grandmother had died from a similar lump that she had discovered when just my age. As yet it didn't inconvenience me or give pain, but I recognised the symptoms and accepted that soon it would, and acknowledged that my life was now under a sentence of death.

Thomas was determined I see a specialist to discover what could be done, and he'd paid what I considered an excessive amount, only to receive the same verdict as my rural doctor gave. I asked how long they thought I would have left; six months at the most the city man said. As long as you need, said my own doctor. I needed at least that amount of time, as Elspbeth and Thomas were expecting their first baby in the summer, and I so much wanted to hold that child in my arms. It would be my third grandchild, but the only one I would ever see.

I had been fortunate in Thomas's choice of bride: I had loved her from first we'd met. A fresh-faced country girl, she had followed in my steps, and had journeyed alone to Canada from her Derbyshire village to marry my son. Unlike my arrival, she had found him waiting for her at the dockside, and they had travelled together across the wide expanse of country on the Pacific Rail. The abattoir was doing well, and she had a nice home waiting for her in Vancouver. Lacking my impulsiveness she had been sensible enough to give Thomas time to prepare for her coming.

She was to prove to be a blessing to me, and I thought of her as my daughter. She reminded me of my own dear Lizzie who would have been of a similar age if she had been allowed to live. My thoughts were often on the three of them, long gone, but never far from my mind. I liked to think of little Tom, grown tall and handsome like his younger brother Thomas, and my poor baby who never got the chance to grow. My children had been lost to me, but I felt myself lucky to have my son and his wife living within travelling distance of the lake, and now that they had a vehicle, were regular visitors.

When I'd first receiving the specialist's verdict Elspbeth and Thomas had immediately offered their home and care. I was touched by their concern but knew instinctively that the one place where I would want to spend my final days would be in my own home, in a much loved house overlooking my beloved lake. They both accepted my decision, but made me promise to have them close when nearing the end.

Hearing of my affliction, Edward had written an emotional letter to tell me of his sadness, and his sorrow that we had never been reunited. But he wrote that he had never forgotten me, and despite the loving care his aunt and uncle had always shown him, nothing had ever replaced me in his heart. I wept at his words, and thought myself well blessed to have such a constant love. Despite the anguish of not being able to comfort him, I was content in knowing that he was happily married with his own family, and was fulfilled farming the land that my father had so cherished.

My husband had been very subdued since learning of my fate, and I believe Thomas had strong words with him as to my care. Fortunately he was involved in a haulage contract which kept him away from home for a considerable time, allowing me to come to terms with my future demise at my own pace, and in solitude. I had no fear of dying, and near the end would put my faith in God.

A part of me eagerly welcomed it, and when having my evening vigil with Mac at the lakeside I couldn't deny my jubilation at the thought of us soon being together again. He had been faithful, and waited such a long time for me to join him.

Lake Solitude. 30th of March 1934.

The End of a Marriage

Art packed up and left me yesterday. He took his belongings and the truck, and walked out of our marriage.

I felt no grief at its ending, only a great relief that he had gone from my life. It had been a disastrous marriage from the very start, and I as much to blame as him. The ending when it came was stark and brief, we had bickered for most of the time we were wed, but the parting came as the result of a bitter row.

He had always been angry at my reluctance to tell him of my finances, and I, much to his fury, would never divulge them. He had seemed content for me to pay the household bills, and to keep him in pocket money, and I had never questioned his own dealings with the bank or demanded he pay his share.

Last year I had sold one of the lakeside cabins, and given the money to Thomas to help finance the abattoir he intended to run. He had seen that there was a need for another slaughterhouse in Vancouver, and had gone into partnership with his employer to open a second one. They had found suitable premises, but lacked the money to equip it. I was reluctant to sell off even the smallest bit of my precious lakeside, but I had wanted to see Thomas established before I died.

The Wiltons had long begged me to sell them a plot, and there would be no other family that I would rather have buy one. We were firm friends and I was godmother to the twins, loving them as if they were my own. When I'd met up with Henry in the city to legalise the deal, I also asked the solicitor to make my two sons the official owners, and holders of the deeds for the remainder of Lake Solitude.

Being unaware of this arrangement, Art had daily pestered me to sell the other cabins, anxious to get his hands on the money. And yesterday, when I'd refused to even discuss the idea he had lost his temper and raged at me – he said he was sick and tired of waiting for me to die. Despite my weakness, I rallied enough to tell him that he was actually better off with me alive, as my boys were now the owners of the lake, and he would be fortunate if Thomas allowed him to stay on here once I'd gone. At first he was struck dumb, and then as his brain registered what I'd done, his fury exploded, he shook me until my teeth rattled and I feared for my life.

He ran like a mad man around the house, gathering his belongings, and some of mine too. And finally he stood at the door and cursed me, saying he hoped I'd have a long and painful death. But before he could

187

close the door and leave I had my retaliation, telling him that I had that morning unknown to him read his tea leaves, and saw only gloom and the hand of the devil at the bottom of his cup, and he would surely be following me to the grave within the year. He came back to my side, and spat in my face, telling me I was a crazy old woman whose prophecies no one believed.

Slamming the door with such a force it broke the glass panel, he then climbed into his truck and raced off down the track, but I had seen the fear in his eyes and I knew he would carry it with him wherever he went.

I'd been shaken by his venom, always aware of the physical violence that he was capable of, but the hatred in his face was quite unnerving. Of late he had been more caring of my welfare, thinking I suppose that I would soon be gone, and he would naturally inherit the lake, which proved to me what I'd always thought; that he didn't marry me out of love, but a calculated greed. And I too had not wed for love, but for the attraction of a handsome face, and the need for companionship. So in the end we both got our just desserts: a partnership that had for both of us been a torment.

A sleepless night had given me time to reflect about our doomed marriage, and my own part in its deterioration. I was not entirely blameless, I had wanted a husband but had not been prepared to share my worldly goods, or to even let go of loving Mac.

But for today I am just glad to be alive, and sitting here on the deck, my eyes observing the peaceful scene that I never tire of viewing, a late spring sun glinting on the clear waters of the lake, birds twittering in the trees and squirrels playing around my feet, and most of all enjoying the utter solitude from which the lake deservedly got its name. I am truly well blessed, and thankfully Art had gone from my life for ever.

Lake Solitude. 1st of May 1934.

Catching Up

My sister Lucy had always been a regular correspondent since I had first left England: she would write me long gossipy letters that had kept me in touch with village affairs, and family news.

She was herself recently widowed, having had a long and happy marriage to the local vet; she had four children, plus numerous grandchildren whom I'd lost count of. She often wrote that she envied me my varied life and travel, but in truth I sometimes envied her, thinking her fortunate to have found the man she loved at an early age. They had been sweethearts whilst still at school, and had married as soon as John had taken over his father's veterinary practice. She still lived in the ivy-covered house that they had moved into the day they married. I remembered it well: a substantial village house, with a large walled garden from which my two brothers would steal plums on their way home from school. I cautioned her not to have regrets as she'd had a fortunate life.

It was Lucy who first wrote of my brother's death in early spring. A blessed release she'd said, he had been crippled with arthritis for a long time, and was in his later years in severe pain. She wrote that Edward and Thomas had been a great comfort to him, and he'd told her just before he died that he had always carried some guilt about keeping the boys from me, and he had encouraged Thomas to travel to Canada, hoping it would give me some solace. I wept at these words, knowing he had been a wonderful surrogate father to both of them.

So now from my mother's five children there was just Lucy and I left. Our sister Matilda had died from a miscarriage many years ago, and her widowed husband had long since remarried, and raised a brood of children. And our brother Arnold had never recovered from the gassing he'd received when fighting in the Great War, dying within twelve month of returning home. For years he had promised to come out to Canada to visit me, and had the notion that if he'd liked the country he might take some land himself and stay. The war had changed his plans, and another person I'd loved was snatched away by an utterly futile conflict.

The village churchyard was now the resting place of much of our family, and Lucy tended the graves of our dear ones with tender care. She wrote me once that William's headstone had fallen in disrepair, and I said I would send money to have it put right, but in her next letter she said that Edward had already arranged and paid for a stonemason to repair it. I was pleased that he was respecting his father's grave, despite having little memory of him. I too found it difficult at times to recollect the faces of my loved ones, such a big chasm of experiences had parted me from them, and I had lived in Canada for many more years than I had spent in the village of my birth.

She gossiped that Bridget, our sister-in-law, had baulked at leaving the farmhouse after our brother's death, and Edward and his wife had to very firmly insist on her moving to the cottage in the village that had been my mother's. I had never met Rebecca, my son's wife, but she sounded someone with whom I would have a lot in common. I can imagine the difficulty of sharing a roof with my brother's sour-faced wife, having once been in that position myself.

Without Lucy's letters I would be in total ignorance of the woman my eldest son had married. He was not good at keeping up correspondence, having briefly written to tell me of his engagement, and later his marriage, and had over the years informed me of each subsequent child that followed, but it was left to Lucy to give me the details which I was naturally curious to hear. Rebecca had come down from Yorkshire to teach at the village school, and according to my sister, Edward had been smitten at first sight, but he'd had considerable competition to win her hand, as the local doctor was also hoping to court her, and Lucy had suspected that the vicar was not adverse to her company either. But Edward with his father's charm had prevailed, and vanquished his rivals to take her to the altar.

My sister said that his new wife was a bonny girl of good sense, and although she was city-born had taken to being a farmer's wife like a duck to water. Thomas too had told me that she was strong-willed, and a very capable housekeeper. She herself had written me a brief note when first engaged to Edward, beautifully written in a fine handwriting, and I'd replied wishing her every happiness. I'm sure in her mind she must have thought me a selfish woman, who had abandoned her children to seek her own pleasure. At times I thought this myself, and wondered what life would have been like if I'd stayed and reared my sons as a mother should. I know I would not have been able to give them the advantages that my brother and his wife had given. Despite Thomas's assurances to the contrary I wonder if they had ever resented my leaving them. Although, if I had not returned to Canada, I would never have known Mac, and he was truly the love of my life.

I had not informed Lucy of my sickness, and had asked Edward not to tell her either. She was in poor health herself, and I didn't want her to be needlessly worried. I had told nobody other than my immediate family. A few of the Lake's regular summer visitors were aware that I was not well, and allowed me the peace and quiet that I craved. My only visitors were Thomas and Elspbeth, and on occasion Eunice with her twins, whom she never permitted to overstay their welcome.

Soon the summer visitors would be gone, and the cabins boarded up for winter, and I would have my beloved lake back again. I spent a lot of time daydreaming, sat out on the deck watching the birds swoop low over the water, occasionally dipping their beaks to triumphantly pull out a fish. I reflected that it's only as life is close to ending that you fully realise what a wonder nature is, and to cherish the simple things that are all around us.

I have put my affairs in order, and written letters to Lucy and my sons asking them not to be sad or to mourn my passing, but to be happy for me as I will be meeting the loved ones who have gone before.

Lake Solitude. 30th of August 1934.

Anticipation

I was very happy all summer. I spent long, restful days lying on the deck. Friends visited and cooked me delicious meals, but as the weeks sped by my appetite lessened, and I was content with a cool glass of fresh lemonade. Thomas and Elspbeth came every weekend; she was now big with child, and I worried that the journey in the heat would be harmful, but she insisted on coming, and despite my protests would tidy the house and help me bathe.

Eventually Thomas arranged to let one of the cabins to a pleasant Swedish couple, a rent-free arrangement, in return for their care of me. They were a pleasant pair, newly married, and having only recently arrived in the country. I couldn't pronounce their names and shortened them to Anna and Sev. Her English was very good, but he had none at all and I would rely on her to communicate the jobs that needed doing around the place. She became a great comfort to me, and was not afraid to scold if I ever exerted myself.

Although still fiercely independent I accepted that my strength was failing, and I needed any help I could get. Elspbeth came to the lake to spend a week with me to escape the heat of Vancouver. We became very close, and I showed her my journals and asked her to take care of them when I'd gone. She wept at this, but promised to keep them safe, saying they were a record of pioneer history. I'd never thought of them in that way, they had simply been a great comfort and a companion to me throughout my life in Canada.

And then the news I had been waiting for, a message from Thomas to say that Elspbeth had given birth in the early hours, and they had a beautiful daughter. What joy! I was so grateful that I'd been allowed to live to see my granddaughter. I would have dearly loved to have raced into Vancouver to see her immediately, but had to accept the limitations of my health and contain my impatience for another two weeks, to allow time for Elspbeth's lying in.

When at last they came I couldn't contain my delight, and when Thomas placed his daughter in my arms I felt such bliss I could only look at her in wonder. Awaking from sleep she opened her eyes and stared into my mine, and I gasped in surprise, she had William's beautiful green eyes that were looking at me almost with recognition. None of my children had inherited them, all having my own hazel ones. I was also pleased to see a look of my mother in her face, which gave me much comfort.

The weekend passed all too quickly, and I was loath to see them go. Elspbeth was blooming in motherhood and Thomas bursting with pride whenever he looked at his daughter. They had named her Elizabeth for Elspbeth's mother, and also for my little Lizzie who had also been christened Elizabeth all those years ago.

I was sad to wave goodbye, and although they promised to come again the following week, I knew that this was our final farewell. I had held Thomas tight and told him I loved him, and kissed Elspbeth and the baby, wishing them both well. I was content now. I had seen the beginning of a new generation, and had held and blessed her, realising that as yet she was the first and only real Canadian in the family.

The fall had come early and although the days were still warm I felt a chill when I lay out on the deck. I would ask Anne to wrap a blanket around me as I wanted to spend my last days out in the open. The local doctor came to see me, held my hand and asked if I was ready. I nodded, and thanked him for his care. I had made my decision many weeks ago and knew exactly what I'd planned.

This last day I have sent Anne and Sev to Vancouver to take a letter to my solicitor, and one to my son, and have persuaded them to accept my offer of staying overnight to explore the city. They were reluctant to leave me, but I insisted that the letters were important. After they left I unlocked the tin trunk and re-read my journals, and for a time I felt young again and relived my life on the prairies. Soon I will finish this, my final entry, and lock it away with the others, allowing Elspbeth to do with them as she feels needful.

I'm feeling weak and very weary, but know that for now I still have the will to carry out my plan. I have taken a large dose of laudanum, and will sit outside for a while until it's time to meet Mac at the lakeside. The drug will dull the pain, and allow my mind to wander whilst I wait.

For a time I found myself back in Derbyshire, running through the meadows with my sister, pulling a ribbon from her hair and tempting her to catch me to get it back; I smiled at such childish pleasures. I had fleeting glimpses of shadowy people who had left my life long ago. And yet it seemed just yesterday when I had got off that train in Blue River Halt and waited for William. And I could still visualise Mac striding down the rail track and into my life. I reflected how wonderful life could be, and how strong a spirit was that it could overcome tragedy and still find happiness.

When night falls I'm going down to the lake to meet Mac, and this time I shall not come back, I shall walk into the clear water until it lifts me up into Mac's waiting arms. And then, as he often said, we shall soar away together and never be parted again.

With anticipation giving me strength I will now put away this last journal into my old tin box, and prepare myself in a truly joyful state of mind, to meet my love again.

Lake Solitude. 13th of September 1938.

A Letter to My Grandma

Derbyshire, England. 2009.

Dear Grandma Jerram,

It feels very strange to be writing a letter to someone I never met, and who no longer exists. I'm unsure how to address you, but you were my grandmother and we once shared a surname, so I feel it appropriate to call you Grandma Jerram.

As I write I suddenly realise that you were totally unaware of my existence. I was born just two weeks before your death, and you would not have received my father's letter telling you of my arrival. Your sister, great-aunt Lucy, became my surrogate grandmother, and she often talked of you, and said she could see a strong resemblance between us, not so much in looks, but in temperament, as I was impulsive and headstrong too. In spite of her poor health she lived to reach a ripe old age, dying a few weeks after her 90th birthday. She was dearly loved, and had been a great comfort to me and my sisters when our mother, Rebecca, died whilst I was still a baby. Our father remarried two years later, and we have three half-brothers, who since my father's death run the family farm together.

We were all reared in the farmhouse that was your childhood home, and played in the same fields that you remembered so well. Close by is the small village churchyard where our loved ones lie. I keep the graves tidy, and always make sure that Grandad Jerram's grave has fresh flowers.

Despite you never having any knowledge of me I have learnt much about you, and your life in Canada. I recently visited my cousins in Vancouver; travel now is so much quicker and easier than it was in your day, and our extended family are in much closer communication.

I stayed with Cousin Eddie who is Thomas's son, born two years after your death. Uncle Thomas is retired and living on Vancouver Island with Aunt Elspbeth, and my cousin Elizabeth is a teacher in Quebec. Cousin Eddie lives in the house that he was born in, and it was whilst staying there that he took me up to the attic and showed me the tin box that still contained your journals. Aunt Elspbeth had placed them there after she had helped clear your house at Lake Solitude, and there they have lain until Cousin Eddie and I carried them downstairs and started to read them. We were both enthralled by their contents, and felt as if we had suddenly become part of your life, and for the first time I missed you, and regretted your loss.

As I read on I began to visualise you as a real person, and felt an instant recognition of our kinship. I was very moved as I scanned your neat handwriting, and began to really feel your presence. The faded pages allowed me to see your growth from an impulsive country girl to the mature, strong woman that you became, who adapted to the hard prairie life, and who survived so much sadness. Alongside the journals were old photographs and for the first time I was able to see your likeness, and also that of Grandfather William.

Whilst in Canada I visited the prairie barn where you married him, and also saw many small windswept cemeteries which bore testimony to the tragedies and hardships of those early pioneer days. I went to Blue River Halt, and whilst surveying its vista of endless prairie imagined how scared you must have been when you first arrived there and found no William waiting for you. I walked the platform of the wooden station house where you fell in love at first sight with Mac, your second husband as he walked up the rail tracks laden with furs. You and he were the first couple to marry there. Surprisingly, the station house has not changed at all from the sketch of it that you did in 1908.

I have also seen the beautiful Lake Solitude which you loved so much, and where you lived unhappily with your third husband, and felt glad for you that you'd had so much happiness, in your previous marriage. I have a photograph of your gravestone, but can never think of it as your final resting place, instead I visualise your spirit roaming free across your beloved prairies.

I'm so glad you kept a journal: you left a legacy that is both a history of that pioneer period, and also a testament of your spirit of adventure. As a child I had known of relatives in Canada, but with the carelessness of youth never gave them much thought. However, when I reached maturity I began to feel curious about my unknown Canadian family, and became determined to visit and repair the broken fragments of our extended relationships. And on this visit I gained more information about you, and became more aware of the gap in my life that your absence had left.

Cousin Eddie told me that your third husband, Art Dunning, had fulfilled your prophecy by dying of a brain haemorrhage within six months of your own death. The following year Uncle Thomas, after consulting my father, decided to sell Lake Solitude. He was advised to divide it up into separate lots, and they sold very quickly, mostly to people who had been regular summer visitors there.

Your house and a small plot of land was sold to an elderly couple, who only lived there for a short time before putting it back on the market, privately telling friends that they had loved it at first, but had become uncomfortable and nervous, saying that they had regularly heard voices at dusk by the lakeside, and yet on investigation found no one there. The plot gained a reputation of being haunted, and the eerie early morning mists seemed to produce phantom shapes, that deceived the eye into believing it something more sinister. I think this hysteria would have amused you, and I can well believe that you and Mac were simply stopping by, keeping a close watch on your beloved lake.

Today these same lakeside plots sell for thousands of dollars, the area becoming known as a millionaire's paradise. Art Dunning was right when he said it was a tidy property that would rise in value. Although, after reading your journals, I think that to you it was always valuable not in monetary terms, but in the peace and beauty that you found there.

I hope that you would forgive me for writing about your life in Canada. Intrigued by the daily entries in your journal I was bold enough to weave stories around them. At times when writing I almost felt you at my shoulder, and as I wrote I wept with you for all your tragedies, and was equally overjoyed at your good fortune. In fact I feel so close to you that I no longer have regrets about our never meeting, and through our shared experiences feel we have crossed the gulf of time.

I have almost finished my writing, and know that I will feel some loss at your final departure from my pen. I hope that you would have approved of the liberties I have taken with your prose and verse, and would appreciate that long after your passing, you still remain very much alive in your granddaughter's heart and mind.

Rest in peace, Grandma Jerram.

Love from your granddaughter, Rita Jerram. X.

Illustrations

The illustrations that follow are reproductions of old family photographs and include sample pages from Edith's journal.

Edith and William Jerram

Grandma Jerram in British Columbia

CNR STATION, BLUE RIVER, B.C.

Grandma in the UK

Mac in France

Grandma and Art

Grandma at Lake Solitude

and wild cherries which made good jelly.
The ground was sand & in a dry season
crops were a failure. One thing greatly
puzzled me at first, one kept living but
hardly ever saw money. Farmers booked
up at the store, & paid when the crops were
sold. If a man wanted a horse, he bought
on time, or exchanged other stock for it.
If a farmer called a sale, others who bought
gave a note to pay in a given time, which a
friend had to back, & it was marvellous
how recklessly these men backed each others
notes. Heavy interest, generally 8% had to be
paid on those notes. No wonder the farmers
went broke. All around the
neighbourhood for miles were empty deserted
homesteads. People had come with their
little capital, built a house & started farming,
full of hope. Three crop failures in succession
deprived them of all they possessed, and
they departed, dejected & broken. A free
homestead of 160 acres of land (sand) is
not worth 2 acres of good ground at home.
Of course stock could be branded & turned
out on the open prairie, where they could
roam for miles. Anything not branded

Page 6 of the journal

6

can be claimed by any one — A farmer pays
a small sum for a brand for his own exclusive
use. No one else can imitate it. I believe ours
was two U's and a bar = ⅄. That means two
irons, one with U & one with the bar. Twice a
year, Spring & Fall, cattle are driven in from
the Prairie into a large fenced in yard called
a Corrall. A fire is built & the irons heated.
Then the young ones are roped & the brand
pressed on their sides — It seems cruel & they
holler awfully — They are sore for some days,
then the scab peels off, & the brand is there
for always — Young calves get the top of their
heads caustised where the horns should
grow: this prevents the horns forming, and
is better in a country where cattle have
to be shipped by train.

What lovely skies were those of Alberta.
Never did I see such glorious sunsets.
The sky seemed one mass of glorious
scintillating colours, which, reflected in
the waters of the lake, defies description.
That first Fall I saw what I had often
read about but never seen, the Aurora
Borealis or Northern Lights said to be
reflection from the icebergs — I went

205

Other novels, novellas and short story collections available from Stairwell Books and Fighting Cock Press

Carol's Christmas	N.E. David
Feria	N.E. David
A Day at the Races	N.E. David
Running With Butterflies	John Walford
Poison Pen	P J Quinn
Wine Dark, Sea Blue	A.L. Michael
Skydive	Andrew Brown
Close Disharmony	P J Quinn
When the Crow Cries	Maxine Ridge
The Geology of Desire	Clint Wastling
Homelands	Shaunna Harper
Border 7	Pauline Kirk
Here in the Cull Valley	John Wheatcroft
How to be a Man	Alan Smith
A Multitude of Things	David Clegg
Know Thyself	Lance Clarke
Thinking of You Always	Lewis Hill
Rapeseed	Alwyn Marriage
A Shadow in My Life	Rita Jerram
Tyrants Rex	Clint Wastling
Abernathy	Claire Patel-Campbell
The Go-to Guy	Neal Hardin
The Martyrdoms at Clifford's Tower 1190 and 1537	John Rayne-Davis
Return of the Mantra	Susie Williamson
Poetic Justice	PJ Quinn
Something I Need to Tell You	William Thirsk-Gaskill
On Suicide Bridge	Tom Dixon
Looking for Githa	Pat Riley
Connecting North	Thelma Laycock

For further information please contact rose@stairwellbooks.com

www.stairwellbooks.co.uk

@stairwellbooks

Recent Fighting Cock Press publications:

Fosdyke and Me And Other Poems	John Gilham (with Stairwell Books)
Temporary Safety	Rose Drew
Dune Fox and Other Poems	Colin Speakman
Beyond the Window	Alan Gillott
Fishing for Spring	Mary Sheepshanks
Dancing blues to Skylarks	Mary Sheepshanks

For further information see www.fightingcockpress.co.uk